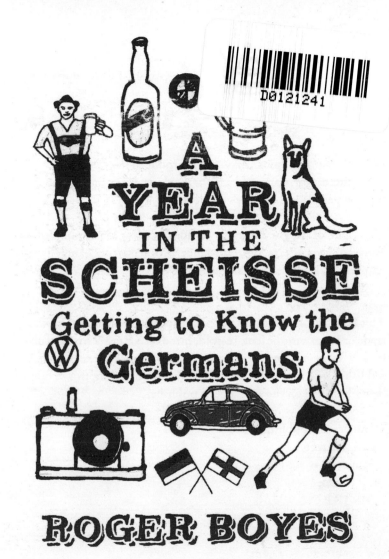

A YEAR IN THE SCHEISSE

Getting to Know the Germans

ROGER BOYES

summersdale

A YEAR IN THE SCHEISSE
Copyright © by Ullstein Buchverlage GmbH, Berlin. Published in
2006 by Ullstein Taschenbuch Verlag

Summersdale Publishers Ltd
46 West Street
Chichester
West Sussex
PO19 1RP
UK

www.summersdale.com

Printed and bound in Great Britain

ISBN: 1-84024-648-0
ISBN 13: 978-1-84024-648-3

A YEAR IN THE SCHEISSE

Getting to Know the Germans

ROGER BOYES

This version is for Ruth and the Dartmoor gang

Contents

Chapter One

The Clash of Civilisations

✉

YOU LOOKING PALE

The SMS pinged onto my tired mobile at the very moment that I entered Germany.

'Turn it off, please,' said the customs officer, a young man with iron-rimmed glasses, more poet than policeman in his soft features. My passport was curled at the edges like stale bread and so the officer had to type in my data rather than swipe it through the machine. He bit his tongue with concentration. The queue was growing impatient. He was a very slow poet. Often, these are the best.

Ping!

✉

TELL HIM YOU DOCTOR

'I must ask you to switch off the phone,' said the officer, very firmly.

'I'm a doctor!' I lied, obeying my electronic orders.

'It says here you're a journalist.' Suddenly alert.

'Well. I'm both. Like, like, er, Chekhov.'

'Chekhov wrote for newspapers?'

I nodded hard. Thinking: did he?

'That's why my phone has to stay on. Could be an emergency.'

'And is there one?'

'You could say so.'

My emergency had a name: Harry. He had managed, probably through bribery, to gain access to a gallery overlooking the whole of the customs and luggage area. It was probably reserved for the anti-terror squad, entry limited to those with legally registered firearms and bulletproof vests. He waved to me as I passed from the increasingly confused poet-policeman to the luggage carousel which was burping and stop-starting like a drunk.

'Give me five minutes,' I mouthed to him, punching the air with an open, splayed hand.

The trolleys, elegantly designed by an award-winning mobility-artist, proved to be useless. Each demanded a one euro coin before it could be unchained. As the plane had just landed from London, only the most thoroughly prepared passengers were able to load their luggage. An American rock band, three white-vested men with key chains round their necks, boxer shorts on display, cursed as they hoisted their guitars and sound systems off the conveyer belt. An Arab solved the luggage problem by handing his cases to his wife. No doubt he had a bad back. Everywhere, there was a huffing and puffing as non-eurozone passengers struggled to cope with entry to Germany. Carefully, I extracted a 15 Turkish lira coin and inserted it into the slot. Harry had first given me the tip and I used the coin, a perfect fit, every time I passed through Berlin airport. With luck the almost worthless Turkish coin would soon be buying me some preternaturally cheap cigarettes from a slot-machine.

It had been a bumpy early morning flight from London on Breezy Airlines, the airborne equivalent of a cattle truck. Nobody vomited. As the passengers milled round the trolleys, as tightly locked as chastity belts, their faces radiated an aquarium-green. Harry's text message could have been sent to any of them: there was a special bargain-airline pallor. They were for the most part sufferers from the easyJet delusion, people who thought that cheap air fares made it possible to be happy in two cities simultaneously. Or that misery in London could be compensated by personal success in Berlin. Or vice versa. Or that there were two levels of happiness, a British brand and a German one; a €29 flight – no meal, no sick bag, no seat number – could somehow complete the individual.

It was Laptop Man that chose to believe this silliness, above all German men who were born in the second half of the 1960s. They had been brought up with the very best medical treatment, they were well fed, pumped up with vitamins, most had never had to wear uniform; there was not a single product of an unwanted pregnancy. Their first instinct on arriving at a new place was to search for a power-point; their actual locus, their habitat, was irrelevant. For them, the Fatherland was not Germany, it was some form of flag-less electronic terrain, limbo *über alles*. That was not my tribe. Germany had, against all the odds, become my adopted Fatherland. The British, of course, have neither a Fatherland nor a Motherland. They say *home*. We're going home for Christmas. It is a word that carries a sense of warmth – of cracking chestnuts round the wood fire – but which has only a limited validity. Home can also be no more than an airless overheated living room. There is nothing grand about it, nothing worth fighting for. Britain as a country is too confused, too busy, too fiddly, too cheapskate, too fraudulent to be considered a Fatherland.

Against all the odds and by default, Berlin had become a place of refuge. It was the place where, after decades of covering revolutions and little, unnoticed wars, I had ended up. Could I perhaps end up liking the country? It seemed improbable. But then, the Germans themselves did not much like it either – least of all the Laptop Man, whose main demand of his Fatherland was: where can I plug in my computer?

Sweating a little, I picked up my bags. I had stuffed them full of Marks and Spencer Cornish Pasties, Cheddar cheese, golden syrup and treacle tart. I had just returned from a 'chat' with my editor, traditionally a time to stock up with foodstuffs unavailable in Germany. You entered the office, kissed the rings of the powerful, and counted the minutes before you could flee for Selfridges Food Hall. It was time, the editor told me, for a more modern approach to Germany. I thought about this for a while, nodded sagely as if confronted by a startling new concept. And tried irony. 'So... fewer stories about Albrecht Dürer?' 'That's it,' he agreed enthusiastically. 'Less culture! Think of our younger readers.' There was a pause while I tried to picture a young reader, sipping a caffè latte in Starbucks, listening to his iPod, flicking through the newspaper with its increasingly big photographs and shrinking texts. 'Articles about cannibals and crime then?' My editor glared at me as if I were a particularly slow pupil. 'And Hitler, of course,' he said, looking at his watch. 'Of course,' I said, 'of course.'

It was fitting, then, that I was driving straight from Berlin-Schoenefeld – a big empty parade ground of an airport – to an auction where perhaps, just perhaps, a watercolour painting by the Führer would be coming up for sale. Harry had got wind of it through an Internet site that specialised in selling Hitler's writing paper, his badges and indeed anything he had ever touched. It was forbidden to sell the stuff in Germany but there were always back-channels. Our destination was a manor house in Saxony. The original owners, inbred aristocrats, had decided to sell the contents. Somewhere, buried among the ancestral finds, there was a tree and a grey sky daubed by the artistically incompetent man from Braunau am Inn. Collectors knew; the auctioneers did not. Was that a journalistically interesting mission? Apparently so.

'You're late,' complained Harry, when I eventually struggled out with my luggage into anaemic sunshine. 'We're supposed to be there by twelve noon sharp.' Harry was a journalistic buccaneer but he was obsessively punctual. He slept with an alarm clock, a mobile programmed to make the sound of a rooster at the appointed hour and a radio that switched on the BBC World Service at eardrum-busting volumes. People who live on their wits rarely leave things to chance. And we were late.

'The car's outside,' said Tony, taking one of the bags. The three of us were the backbone of the British press corps. No cliché about Germany left the country without at the least one of us having given it our seal of approval. The physical contrast between Harry and Tony was striking, they could have performed in a version of *The Odd Couple*. Harry was solid, robust, built like a chest of drawers; his face was flushed, his hair receding, his brown military moustache trimmed to make him resemble Ernest Hemingway in the days when the writer was in Spain reporting on the civil war. Tony was gaunt, a face etched with worry as if he had been a schoolteacher for too long. The bane of his life was his wife Roberta who, having realised early on that she had married the wrong man, had made it her life's mission to change Tony.

It was a relief to be back in the embrace of colleagues. A visit to the newspaper always left me feeling under the weather, as if I was about to come down with bronchitis; it depressed the immune system. Being on the road was liberation. An illusion, of course.

Harry programmed the GPS as Tony and I stashed the luggage.

'Bloody machine doesn't recognise the DDR,' cursed Harry, feeding in different variants of the Saxon town that was supposed to be our destination.

'We don't call it that anymore. Communism collapsed, remember?' said Tony and turned round from the front seat to hiss at me. 'Did you bring the steak and kidney pie?'

I nodded. Roberta had put the whole of his family – that is, Tony and their twin sons – on a vegetarian diet, having read that meat-free meals improved school performance. As a result Tony was constantly popping out of his apartment on one pretence or another in order to binge on curry wurst. His favourite forbidden food, however, was steak and kidney pie. I had brought six with me in the hope that it would lighten up Tony's perpetual gloom.

'Off we go!' announced Harry, stepping hard on the accelerator.

'Take-the-next-turning-right!' The voice of the navigation system had the steely ring of Margaret Thatcher. It was not a tolerant voice; it was the tone of a finger-wagging supernanny who refused even to consider the possibility of resistance from the children in her charge. One sensed immediately that she believed in corporal punishment.

'Oh, shut up,' grumbled Tony, talking to the machine. 'Maggie Thatcher was always wrong. If we follow her guidance we will end up completely lost.'

'Yeah, stupid woman,' I chipped in. It was Thatcher who had driven many of us to become foreign exiles. Britain had become a colder place; solidarity had crumbled, and the pursuit of money had somehow become confused with the pursuit of happiness. For all its faults, Germany still believed in Fair Play.

'Just leave her alone,' said Harry, 'she was a great leader.' Harry had got a special deal on his second-hand Mercedes S-Klasse. Although it had seats that massaged the lower back, it had been missing a navigation system, raising suspicions that the car might have had a dubious past. Since Harry's German was a little shaky, and since he had never had a nanny, he invested in a British GPS machine.

'Take-a-left-turn-now!' said the Thatcher clone.

We laughed.

That was a mistake.

Tony and I, both not wearing our seatbelts, were thrown forward as the car skidded, brakes squealing. On Harry's side there was a sickening thud and, as we came to a halt, an airbag belatedly started to balloon up, pushing the wind out of him.

'Are you all right, Harry?' asked Tony. His airbag had not functioned at all.

'I feel as if I'm being raped by a hippo,' said Harry very slowly, measuring out his breath.

I too was dazed. Outside our windows a group of young people had gathered and were silently explaining to each other what had happened. They were semaphoring to each other. One teenager curled his hand into a fist and then smashed it into his palm. Yes, that is what must have happened: we had been hit by a car.

'Have we gone to heaven?' I asked. That was how it seemed; a heaven encircled by silent, gesticulating angels.

All three of us staggered out of the Mercedes, Harry wriggling through Tony's door (his was too buckled, jammed shut as if by a steam press). We were gasping for air, as pale as bedsheets, wobbly at the knees.

'It was that swine,' said Tony, pointing to the cream-coloured taxi that had rammed us.

Harry strode over to the driver. Or at least he *imagined* that he was striding – Gary Cooper in some 1950s Western in search of justice. In fact, he was rocking from foot to foot and he was shaking all over.

'You dammed fool!' he shouted. It came out in a high-pitched way, with a hysterical edge. 'We had the right of way!'

'English, eh! No wonder you drive on the wrong side of the road! Cretin!' The taxi driver had the face of a true Berliner, gnarled like a potato. His toupee was askew.

'I want your insurance details right now, you shirt-lifter.' Harry must have drawn conclusions from the man's toupee.

'*Du Schlappschwanz!*' The German's response was equally physical: 'You drooping prick!'

'Pillow-biter!'

The wordless angels were watching aghast. I realised why they were there: not divine intervention but rather a secret decision by the notoriously eccentric Berlin Senate. It had offered deaf people in Berlin subsidised rents to live near Schoenefeld as part of a long-term plan to introduce night flights and make the airport into the new Heathrow. The kids must have been locals, out for a day of planespotting. Now they had a chance to lip-read some of the rudest words in the English and German language.

'We should stop this,' I told Tony, who was drinking from a bottle of water.

'Maybe all three of us should confront this ugly bugger,' he said. 'A show of force is called for.' I took a closer look at Tony. None of us was injured but he, like Harry, was shaking. Wellington, before going into battle against Napoleon, took one look at his own soldiers and declared: 'They may not frighten the French, but by God they frighten me!' That was our predicament. Three unsteady Englishmen were no match for a robust and angry Berliner. Still, in the name of British honour, we had to give it a try. The deaf teenage angels followed us with their eyes as we trooped over to the taxi with pathetically clenched fists.

'Get out of your idiotic car!' boomed Tony. Or perhaps it was more like a squeal.

A vein twitched in the driver's bull neck. He looked at us silently. And sneered.

'Beat yourselves up, you wankers. I don't have time,' said the driver in his broad Berlin dialect before reversing quickly. He spat out of the window in a great phlegmatic dollop, narrowly missing Tony.

'Shit,' said Harry.

'Shit,' said Tony.

Thank God, I thought.

At that moment, my mobile rang. I picked it up, not recognising the number.

'Hello son,' came a dimly-familiar voice. 'I'm not ringing at a bad time, am I?'

Chapter Two

A German Biography

There was a chicken on the kitchen table, quietly awaiting its time in the oven. I had been in a daze since the minor crash at the airport. My hearing was fuzzy as if I were holding my breath in a chlorinated swimming pool. My throat was dry and little blue flashes would sometimes dart in front of my eyes. The only sense that was still functioning normally was my appetite. I had been eating double breakfasts and triple lunches. Harry ruled out the possibility of pregnancy – 'Believe me,' he said, with absolute conviction – so I put my feelings down to delayed shock. We abandoned our Hitler-treasure-hunt after the collision, which was just as well since it turned out that the signature on the suspected Führer painting was A. R. not A. H. It sold for forty euros after the auctioneer hinted that A. R. was probably the unhappy, and certainly untalented, governess of the aristocratic Saxons.

'Look at it this way,' said Tony, as I helped to hide his steak and kidney pies in the golf bag that he kept in his cellar. 'We didn't waste a day.'

'We could have scratched the "R" until it became a "H",' grumbled Harry. A bulge the size of a pigeon's egg had taken shape on his forehead. The car was out of action for a day or two. 'If I ever see that man again, I'll strangle him with my bare hands.' I looked at Harry's hands. They were indeed the hands of a strangler.

We agreed to meet later in the week: another Führer story was looming. For the time being, though, I could concentrate on preparing a culinary surprise for Frau Beckenbender, my guru in all matters German. I felt sure she would approve my choice of bird.

There was a paper sticker on the bird's bottom, the official government-ordered certificate of origin. It read, 'Höllenhund Farm. From birth to slaughter, this chicken is a purely German product.'

Underneath this was a checklist:

Parents: Deutsch
Birth: Deutsch
Feed: Deutsch
Slaughter: Deutsch

So much for the dream of a multicultural society. Couldn't at least one of the parents have been Greek or Swedish? There was an attractive simplicity to the life of a chicken that was resolutely Deutsch from birth to death, from hatched egg to roasted Christmas. How much more complicated was the CV of a middle-aged journalist. The telephone call from my father had disturbed me. He rarely used the telephone, preferring to write three letters a year, long philosophical ruminations about a past that was so much slower and more dignified than the shabby commercialised present. Acceleration, for Dad, was the root of all evil; not money, passion or reality television, or any of the usual suspects, but rather the mindless hunt for ways to stretch or cheat time. He would fly into a rage at the sight of a young man talking on a mobile phone while driving a car. If the man also wore a gold chain and sunglasses, the rage became a tempest of almost Biblical dimensions. A faster world banished reflection, ate away at the individual, made for bad decisions, poor concentration and a frenzied search for sensation. 'I should have been mummified in 1945,' he would say. To which I would reply: '1945 was better than 1946?' And then the lament would begin. For Britain, success on the battlefield or the sportsfield was always a prelude to failure and steep decline. The beginning of the end of English football, my father would argue, was England's Wembley victory over West Germany in 1966.

That was the tone of his letters, written in spidery ink on the occasion of my birthday, Christmas and, for some obscure reason, his wedding anniversary. (Was my mother perhaps pregnant at the altar? The numbers added up.) These letters never failed to cheer me up. Dad seemed to have no need to communicate in between letters and when I told him he was free to ring me on my mobile, he merely scoffed: 'Mobile phones! The tool of the Devil!' So the phone call at the airport took me by surprise, and not only because I was surrounded by deaf angels. Something mysterious was going on and I was determined to ask Frau Beckenbender about it. She was roughly the same generation as Dad and we had talked about him in the past. When I was a student in Germany she had been not only my landlady but also my language instructor and my life-coach. English children of my class were sent to boarding school to make them independent; they ended up estranged from their parents and dependent on institutions to plonk food in front of them and sort out their laundry. Frau Beckenbender had been a young girl when she fled from the east. Her mother had suffered a nervous collapse on the trek westwards and she was a master of all the things at which I was incompetent. Now she was coming to dinner and I was determined, in my cack-handed fashion, to impress her with my cooking skills.

Two cookbooks, one English, one German, were propped up on the kitchen window sill. I strained to read the small script. The recipes seemed so lacking in elan. Kohlroulade – or in the English version, stuffed cabbage – looked tasty enough but so utterly predictable. The plump blonde chicken offered opportunities for new culinary adventure. Why not stuff the chicken with cabbage? And perhaps a few prunes? If nothing else it would be extremely healthy. Frau Beckenbender, who used to take the waters in Bad Oeynhausen every year, would surely appreciate it. I basted the chicken, listening to a heavy-fisted rendition of Chopin on the radio, and then gently slipped the bird into the oven. I set the timer – Ding! – and put the cabbage on to boil. Then – driiing, driiing! – the phone rang.
  'Am I disturbing you?'
  I sighed.
  'No, Dad, just cooking.'
  'You're a busy man.'

'What's up? Is something wrong?' The timbre of my father's voice had changed. It seemed to have lost the parade-ground manner, the authoritative briskness.

'Er, no, nothing. Just checking how you are.'

'But you never call.'

There was a silence on the line. Extracting information from my father was like trying to prise a ten euro note out of the clenched first of a Swabian or a fiver from a Scotsman.

'Dad? Dad? Are you still there?'

'Aye. What's that infernal row in the background?'

'Chopin.' I switched off the radio. 'No, the extractor fan.' The cabbage was making its presence known.

I moved with the phone to the toilet, which smelled of chemically-synthesised lavender (but somehow better than the cabbage), and shut the door.

'That's better, I can hear you now.'

'So what's bothering you?'

'It's just… the cleaning lady.'

I felt a dull throb of anxiety, a migraine brewing behind my eyes. My father was at constant war with Meryl, his irritatingly cheerful home help, who came in for ironing and to dust the mantelpiece. For the last eight years he had suspected her of stealing three pound coins from his emergency cash reserve stored in an old Nescafé tin. It was his distrust and simulated hatred of Meryl that kept him alive.

'What about her?'

'She's not coming any more.'

'Oh, God, Dad. Whatever you said to her, apologise right now.'

'She says I haven't paid her.'

'And? Have you?'

'No, honestly, no, I haven't.'

His voice was croaking as if his mouth had been open all night, drained of spittle. Dad had always been difficult. A war hero, he had wanted me to be a soldier or an airman and had insisted that I wear the creases of my trousers so sharp they could cut cheese. When I tried to iron them and singed a hole, he flew into a tantrum. It was not easy to please him.

'How long has it been since you paid her?'

'Don't know.'

'A week? Two weeks?'

Silence again.

'More like three months. The truth is, son, I'm pretty much broke.'

I smothered a laugh. Dad had been claiming poverty since I was in short trousers.

'No, really, I'm serious.' The words came out in a gush now. 'I talked to the bank manager, he says there's nothing left, just the pension and that's barely enough to feed a cat.'

'Dad, no bank ever says you're broke. The less money you have, the more interesting you become to them.'

'They say I've got a big overdraft. The savings have gone. Maybe I'll have to sell my medals.'

'And your premium bonds?'

'Sold them last year to pay for the new television.'

I was losing patience. It was time to check the chicken and the cabbage. A faint whiff of saucepan flambé was reaching me from the kitchen.

'Why the hell did you buy a TV?'

'Because the last one was black and white and exploded when the new vicar came to tea.'

'Look, Dad, can I ring you back another time? Hang on a moment.'

As I suspected, the water had boiled out of the saucepan; the cabbage was charred. I could understand why chefs, even the balding and bulging ones, are considered attractive to women. Their hands have to be everywhere and the act of bringing all the dishes to a climax together is suggestive of skill outside the kitchen. Letting food overcook indicated a broader failure as a man; an incompetent cook was surely a clumsy lover.

'Shit!' I shouted, hastily switching off the oven and wondering whether to throw the cabbage out of the window into the courtyard below to join the various syringes and piles of dog turd. There was a packet of instant mashed potatoes in the cupboard, so a substitute was at hand. Then I remembered my father and picked up the receiver.

'Dad, are you still there? Bit of a crisis here, I'm afraid.'

He hung up, without a word.

There was still time, but not much, to save dinner. Frau Beckenbender was a pedant. She liked to sit down and eat almost immediately after arriving. Small talk was vulgar. Food should be served up and should demand concentration as a sign of respect for the cook. I looked at the chicken carcase and the burned cabbage and shook my head; I was inexplicably angry with my father. Instant mashed potatoes were really not the solution. My relationship with Frau Beckenbender – that is, her role as an informal tutor in all matters German – was based largely on food and its memories. We would sit round her kitchen table in Hamburg, an Anglophile city that had been bombed flat by British pilots like my father. The language books would be open and from the stove would come the smell of potato soup. Whatever text we studied, Frau Beckenbender would return to the subject of the war. It seemed normal to me: the generations of my parents and my grandparents were in constant time-travel, commuting to a past that was more vivid and more real. Sometimes, I thought: war is their drug. It wrecked them physically and mentally but they became hooked on the fear, the intensity of life, the making-do, the warmth. The short-term. For Frau Beckenbender, teaching German to an Englishman was not so much about language, or even culture, but about therapy, about surviving in the absence of a father, about a life centred on the kitchen rather than the living room or the bedroom. I had come to understand her when we had a lesson on cooking vocabulary. Her brown eyes lit up when she described the sixteen dishes that could be made out of potatoes. Suddenly I remembered that my family too had grown up with the memory, real or inherited, of meals based on potatoes, on swedes and turnips. They were war-vegetables and to eat them was a patriotic duty. Great Aunt Mabel would sing to me as a child:

Potatoes new, potatoes old
Potato (in a salad) cold
Potatoes baked or mashed or fried
Potatoes whole, potatoes pied
Enjoy them all, including chips
Remember spuds don't come in ships!

Potatoes were home grown. Neither England nor Germany needed to import them. For the English, potatoes were an act of resistance, they made us less vulnerable to Hitler and his U-boats, which were attacking the food convoys over the Atlantic. For the Germans, potatoes grown in scruffy allotments were an act of independence from rationing Nazis and blockading Russians.

'Seventeen,' I told Frau Beckenbender, remembering a recipe from Great Aunt Mabel for potato fingers. 'You make some mashed potato, add flour, shape them like fingers and put them in an oven.'

'Eighteen,' retorted Frau Beckenbender and gave me the recipe for potato pastry.

Our potato ping-pong continued over the years. By the time I had finished my studies we had reached eighty-nine potato recipes. Now that I was back in Germany, this time as a correspondent, I felt it was time to take our relationship to another level: cabbage. So, no instant potatoes. I had somehow to re-invent burned cabbage as an edible alternative. And time was running out. I wrenched open the fridge: there was some ancient low-fat cream, a jar of capers, a few rashers of bacon and a bottle of chilli. It would just have to do. The bacon was thrown into a pan and deep-fried while I used an old toothbrush to paint the cream on the black bits of the cabbage. The capers were scattered round, the crispy bacon sliced and mixed into the cabbage and three drops of chilli covered up more fire-damage. If in doubt, says one of England's top and relentlessly optimistic chefs, add colour. The doorbell rang and I took one last look at the dish. It was certainly colourful, but then so were car accidents.

Frau Beckenbender stood beaming at the threshold. Her bird-like figure was dwarfed by a huge swollen marrow. 'I thought it was time to move on from our potato obsession,' she said, 'and I have dozens of marrow recipes. But then I caught the smell of cabbage in the courtyard and I know you had the same idea.'

I took the marrow. 'Thank you. Yum-yum. Though I like flowers too you know, Frau Beckenbender. I'm not short of food. Rationing ended a while ago. You can buy all sorts of things in the shops nowadays.'

'You're teasing me.'

'No, really, rationing is over.'

'Rationing is never over,' she said, with a sudden Hanseatic gloom. 'Life is rationing.'

'Well, you can eat as much cabbage as you like today,' I said, quietly admiring my own nerve, 'I've conjured up something very special for you.'

Frau Beckenbender's crinkled face lit up. She handed me her coat and immediately sat down at the kitchen table. 'Cabbage is my favourite.' I believed her because she was in love with the same memory of poverty and deprivation that the rest of my apartment block hated. It was a typical tenement in Berlin's Prenzlauer Berg district, built for workers in the early twentieth century, bombed, refurbished, but still essentially a place for people who counted their money carefully at the end of the month. The neighbours included a car dealer who spent long hours in the solarium, a female teacher who was having an affair with a sixteen-year-old pupil, a Serb who wore false beards (Fridays: black specked with grey; Thursdays: red and bushy) whenever he went to the supermarket for fear of being caught by investigators from the International War Crimes Tribunal. Average Berlin. What they had in common was a distaste for cabbage: it was the smell of social decline. There was no other incident in the daily rhythm of the house that aroused so much collective anger: not the incontinent terrier, not the drunk who rang the doorbells after midnight. Cabbage, however, was a cause for official complaint. The concierge would knock on the door, clear his throat and put in a formal request to open the windows or deodorise the corridor or to stop cooking and eat somewhere else. On one occasion he brought me a voucher for a McDonald's Maxi Meal, sponsored by my neighbours.

'It's delicious,' said Frau Beckenbender, and I wanted to believe her. 'Or at least, interesting.' Potatoes may have evoked her childhood. But cabbage was the aroma of her teenage years. It meant, as she returned from school and edged past the pram in the hallway and as her stomach juices started to gurgle, that her grandmother was home. Frau Beckenbender's mother had lost her sanity during the long flight from the Russians but her grandmother had stayed solid, an East Prussian with a taste for cabbage and meatballs.

'What are the black bits?' asked Frau Beckenbender, unusually talkative.

'It's an Irish recipe,' I said, dodging the question.

'That would explain the chilli.'

We fell into our customary silence. A wave of nausea swept over me as I tried to digest my own incompetent cooking. My dog, Mac, who normally would have been fed under the table with unwanted nuggets, had crept away into the far corner of the apartment.

'Well, that was very good,' said Frau Beckenbender, having polished her plate. 'You must give me the recipe for Irish burned cabbage.'

She did not mention the chicken which had emerged from the oven in an unhealthy-looking brown crust. Surprisingly, Frau Beckenbender turned down my offer of dessert – my speciality, pear flambé – and so we carried the plates to the kitchen and opened the window to clear the smells. The flies stared to buzz in but after a brief reconnaissance flew out again; apparently there was nothing edible. From the courtyard there wafted up fragments of conversation; teenagers talking street slang, addressing each other as 'pizza-face'.

I grimaced and shut the window. This was not Frau Beckenbender's world, not her language.

'Sorry about that. Kids. Different planet.'

'At least they were speaking a kind of German. Better than these managers shouting "task force" or "branding" down their disgusting mobile phones.'

'You sound like my father,' I said, discreetly covering my mobile phone with a dish cloth.

'I think,' said Frau Beckenbender slowly, 'there are probably worse things than sounding like your father.'

And so, over peppermint tea with just a hint of chilli (I had forgotten to wash the spoon), I poured out my worries to Frau Beckenbender. Was my father having a nervous breakdown? Was he trying to tell me something between the lines? What were my duties as a son? Frau Beckebender had a grown up daughter and had very precise ideas about mutual responsibilities. Unfortunately, they were ideas that were first hatched on a rundown pre-war Prussian estate. As usual, she spoke with the authority of a schoolmistress. I did not dare interrupt.

'There comes a time when a parent becomes a child and a child becomes a parent. Sometimes, it is a single moment.

For me, it was when my mother was assaulted by Russian soldiers. I didn't stop wanting to be a child but I had to take on adult responsibilities. That is how it is with your father now. Maybe it is just the beginning of a chain of events whereby he surrenders parental power to you. He sounds like a tired man.'

Frau Beckenbender had never met my father yet in all of our conversations about him she seemed to have developed an intimate understanding of his personality.

'Yes, I suppose he is. But what happens next? Am I to look after him? I have enough problems looking after myself.' Mac, who may or may not have been listening into the conversation, started to choke. I strode over to him and put my hand under his rib cage, pushing upwards. That usually put an end to his panic attacks. But he continued to cough, splutter and retch.

'He's swallowed some of the bacon,' said Frau Beckenbender, 'or a chicken bone.' I held the dog's mouth open with one hand and reached inside the throat with the other. Sure enough, there was a chicken bone mixed with cabbage. I eased it out.

'The Irish recipe?' asked Frau Beckenbender.

'Bloody Irish. How do you know so much about dogs?'

'Grew up with horses.'

'And fathers?'

'As I said, grew up with animals.'

'I don't get it.'

'We follow the rhythms of the animal world, how could it be otherwise? Yes, parents become children and children have to find a way between guilt, responsibility and self-interest – that's human. But the basic truth is that you will have children yourself, grow old and die. Or you won't have children, and you will grow old and die. That's the law of the farmyard.'

'Why do you always cheer me up, Frau Beckenbender?'

The dog had, with a clatter of arthritic joints, just jumped onto the sofa next to her, correctly identifying her as the person who had recently saved his life.

'I'm not a killjoy, you know. Being adult means finding pockets of pleasure and contentment in a life of responsibility. If you don't do that, you condemn yourself to eternal childhood. And you don't want to do that, do you?

'No, I suppose not,' I said sheepishly. Although I was far from sure.

'Remember the old saying – there are only two certainties: death and taxes.'

'To death and taxes,' I said, raising my cup of strange-tasting tea in a mock toast to my elderly guest. The dog burped.

Chapter Three

An Indecent Proposal

'I'm afraid it doesn't look good!'

Dr von Landauer's reedy voice came drifting out of his office. His door, leather-padded to muffle financial secrets, was slightly ajar. The secretary looked disturbed, scratching the inside of her ear with a biro in a most unattractive manner.

'What's that all about?' I asked her, nodding towards the door. We had known each other for some time and I had never seen her so on edge. She took off her Gucci glasses, rubbed her eyes and replaced them. She seized a piece of scrap paper, crumpled it and threw it, with one vaulting movement, into a wastepaper basket. I felt like a student of Dr Freud confronted with an interesting neurological case-study.

'He's expecting you,' she blurted out at last.

'Landauer wants to talk to me?' She gulped. I gulped.

Dr von Landauer was my tax adviser. We had been at university together and he was certainly the most boring of my acquaintances there, unable to drink two beers without reciting some lines of Ovid. It was only after we all graduated that we noticed he had not once, in four years, ever paid for a drink. As a result our whole gang – even Steve, who was beginning to make millions with a website called kill-your-neighbour.com – trusted Dr von Landauer with their money. He may have been a bit strange but he was a genius of sorts. I certainly needed a financial mastermind. Yet another phone call from my father had convinced me that he was destitute. Since I had no brothers or sisters, and since my mother had long since divorced him, my father had become my problem. Plainly I would have to support him for the rest of his life. There was not a booming employment market for ageing bomber pilots. Nowadays bombers tended to strap dynamite under their shirts and blow themselves up at bus stops; not a job with a financial future. As the train rattled from Berlin to Dresden, I tried to make sense of the new situation. The most terrifying option was that my father would come to live with me. That had to be avoided at all costs. I could already picture the daily struggle: his shaving kit laid out in the bathroom like grenadiers awaiting inspection, his model aircraft on the mantelpiece, his cheerful off-key whistling of Rule Britannia as he showered at five o'clock in the morning. Day in, day out: it was a fast track to insanity.

Even the gentler options sent shudders down my spine. Unless he had already sold it, Dad was the proud owner of a Tuareg safari caravan, which was parked in his back garden awaiting some extraordinary adventure. Dad never travelled anywhere in it but used to walk the few yards from the kitchen, past the dahlias, to the blue-and-white caravan and sit quietly, sunk in a dream world, drunk with the possibility of independent travel, bargaining perhaps with Bedouin camel traders or sheltering from the poisonous arrows shot from blow pipes by Congolese pygmies. Now I could see a different future for the little Tuareg safari caravan with its chemical toilet and head-bruising bunk bed. It would be parked outside my Berlin apartment block. In Dad's fantasies, the caravan would give him autonomy. I squeezed my eyes closed and imagined what would happen next. First, he would ring the doorbell for sugar, then to use the toilet – the caravan's sewage system was constantly blocked – then to use the phone, or to complain about the neighbour's cats, or because the heating had broken down. My home, my work and my life would become satellites of my father's caravan.

I needed a quick solution from Dr von Landauer. What does a room in an old people's home actually cost? And even if I could afford it, how was I going to persuade him to live in one, an Englishman among the Huns? It didn't bear thinking about. Out of the window of Dr von Landauer's out-chamber I could see a human centipede of Japanese tourists shuffling towards the Zwinger Palace, Nikon digitals at the ready. They had twenty-five minutes for August the Strong and then it would be back to the coach and on to Prague. I envied them. It was easier, I felt sure, to be an Asian in Europe than an Englishman in Germany; they were protected by a kind of innocence, a special immunity to the European virus.

'Life isn't supposed to be easy, you know,' said the secretary, as if reading my thoughts. Perhaps I had spoken aloud, a further symptom of my mental decay as a journalist. I could see that she was almost in tears. The piggy redness round her eyes, which I had taken to be a dust allergy, was now becoming watery.

'Is anything the matter?' I could not remember her name. Women were so complex.

'In there,' she pointed to the office and broke off her sentence.

I took this to be an invitation to enter Dr von Landauer's sanctum. There was an odd whispering noise coming from the room, which I had earlier taken to be a defective air conditioning machine. A curious smell too, an obscure eau de cologne perhaps, or a Saxon gastronomic delicacy.

The sight that greeted my eyes can only be described as hellish. As a foreign correspondent I had been in some unpleasant situations in the Balkans and other trouble spots. Dante's Hell had flatterers steeped in human excrement, false prophets with their heads on backwards and hypocrites in cloaks made of lead. What terrible sin, then, had von Landauer committed in his earlier life? As I walked in, the tall, distinguished financial adviser to Germany's celebrities, keeper of a thousand secrets, had his hand up the bottom of a black Labrador.

'It doesn't look good at all,' he called out again to his secretary. Slowly it dawned on me that his comment had nothing to do with my financial status.

'Stand still my beauty, this is hurting me more than it is hurting you.' The desk had been cleared of heavy, embossed tomes about EU directives and the ins-and-outs of inheritance. Even the light-up plastic globe showing all member countries of the Tax Accountant Association of the Western Hemisphere, even his precious globe had been shifted onto the floor. The black Labrador, squirming with discomfort, was straddled over the blotting paper while Dr von Landauer burrowed deep inside the animal like a rescue team searching for trapped coalminers. Slowly, very slowly, my accountant's hand, sheathed in a plastic washing-up glove, emerged from the bottom with a soft plop. This surely was a Dante-esque vision: a divine punishment for incompetent accountants.

'Aaah!' said Dr von Landauer.

'Aaah?' I said, a little shy of interrupting this very intimate operation.

'Oh, you're here.'

'Yes, Ingo,' – we had dubbed him 'Bingo' at University because of his ability to juggle numbers – 'we have an appointment. About my finances. I can come back later.' I was groping for words.

'Anal glands,' said Dr von Landauer.

'Ah, yes.'

'Can't live with them, can't live without them.'

Dr von Landauer chuckled to himself. He stripped off the glove and dropped it into the waste paper basket, next to a faded copy of the *Tax Accountant's Bulletin*. 'One hundred tips for clever investors', it said on the front cover.

The accountant smacked the sore bottom of the dog. 'Off you go, Rasputin.' Then, as the dog gambolled stiffly to the door, Ingo raised his voice so that his secretary could hear. 'It's the glands, Julia. You'll have to get rid of them! But don't worry, it'll be painless.'

'She's been worried all day,' said Dr von Landauer, wiping his hands with moist tissues. 'Just make sure he doesn't sit on a damp pavement for a few days.'

Through the open door I could see the secretary, Julia, cradling her dog. They both seemed in need of therapy.

The accountant rubbed his nose with the hand that had recently been on canine safari and started to place his files back on his desk.

'How's Mac?'

'Fine,' I said, hoping the conversation would not turn to Mac's anus.

'Paying dog tax?'

'No, he's an illegal.'

'Well, watch your step. Berlin is training the unemployed to be dog inspectors. Quite tough some of them. Ex-army. Kosovo, that kind of thing. They're setting up a special dog-catchers camp. Every euro counts nowadays.'

At university it was always clear that Ingo wanted to be a vet. His father, however, was paying for his studies – Oxford was not cheap – and insisted that only women should make a profession out of animals. It was Ingo's personal tragedy. Animals were his passion but the rules of his caste were that one did not bring passion to a profession. That was vulgar. 'I'm a vet trapped in the body of an accountant,' he would explain to us. And now, with his father long dead, it was too late to change his life. He expected, though, that all of his clients and his staff should be animal owners. The greatest triumph of his hybrid career so far was to treat the tame but arthritic leopard of an Italian soprano while simultaneously liberating the singer from her duty to pay VAT.

I explained my father's precarious situation and my reluctance to become his carer. Dr von Landauer nodded his head with understanding while fiddling with the computer that had been put back on the desk. He whistled through his teeth.

'I can only repeat: it doesn't look good.'

'No, Ingo, that was Rasputin. I don't, thank God, have a problem with my anal glands.'

'I was talking about you too. Look, your father is broke and old, which means, in the Anglo-Saxon culture, that he has to survive on a state pension that can barely keep a Chihuahua in biscuits. And that means, old chum,' – he said this in English, in what he imagined to be an aristocratic drawl: 'o-l-d c-h-u-m' – 'you have to pick up the bill. How long has he got?'

My chin dropped.

'That's a rather heartless question.'

'Realistic. West-Highland terriers, lifespan fourteen to sixteen years; Dobermans, eight to eleven years; male humans, seventy-three to seventy-seven years; British male humans, sixty-eight to seventy-three. Got to know these things in my business.'

'He was a pilot. Got through the war OK.'

'Ah – the survival gene! You've got him until he's eighty-five. What is he now? Mid-seventies?'

I nodded.

'We're looking at €200,000 in care costs alone. Does he eat a lot?'

'Ingo, this is my father we're talking about, not one of your bloody Dobermans.'

'Calm down, it's just a question of working out how much extra income you will need. Because, quite frankly, you are already living well beyond your means. I was about to send you a letter on this very subject. You're eating in restaurants, taking taxis. These are thin times and you have to adapt.'

'I just want to do my bit to support the Berlin economy.'

'Berlin will go bankrupt with or without your help. It is the last proletarian fortress yet it has no factories. Do you know how many Berliners regularly visit restaurants? Thirty thousand! Out of a population of three million. Why do you think you should belong to the tiny minority and not to the majority? Why don't you learn to cook properly and stay at home more?'

I acknowledged the advice with a sharp nod.

'So what should I do? I mean, apart from starve and travel by tube.'

'Save, save, save. That is the spirit of the times.'

'How?'

'Move your apartment, get out of that ridiculously fashionable slum in Prenzlauer Berg.'

'Actually, I am about to move. To somewhere grander. The newspaper decided I need to live next to the rich and famous.'

'Where exactly?'

'Grunewald. Part of a big old house.'

Von Landauer sighed.

'It won't be cheaper, I take it.'

'No, it won't.' The rent was in fact double what I was paying. 'I thought I could write off the study against taxes. And the sofa where I read newspapers. And the dining room where I cook for politicians.'

'And the lavatory where you flush down the tabloids? And the bedroom where you entertain aspiring film stars? Those times have gone, you know. We live in a cold climate.'

Something cold and wet was pushing at my crotch. It was Rasputin's nose. I pushed him away and immediately felt guilty: the dog, after all, had a sore bottom and was about to lose his anal glands.

'Your fundamental problem is breaking up with Becky. I don't think you understand that a change in lifestyle means a change in financial health.'

'I hardly pay her anything anymore. Becky is about to become a news anchorwoman. Or at least she has applied for the job. They have told her to lose eight kilos.'

'She told me.' Becky, my former wife, had been at university with us.

I suspect, but cannot prove, that she slept with Ingo back then. She was certainly his type: well-bred, horse-loving and overweight. The modern English argot for male bonding based on shared experience of a woman is 'one-away friendship'. I didn't like the idea of being Ingo's one-away chum. He was unorthodox enough already, with his curious mixture of the fiscal and the canine.

'Becky always had a weight problem. She was born with a silver spoon in her mouth and just carried on eating.'

'She seems happy enough now.'

'Yes.' Becky was living with a wiry woman archaeologist who sported a US-marines haircut. 'I want to bear her child,' she had told me recently. Predictably, I asked how this could possibly be arranged and she had glared at me as if I was being deliberately obtuse. 'I'm a Catholic,' she said (which was true), 'I believe in immaculate conception.'

'The point about the divorce,' said Dr von Landauer, speaking in his slow, plodding manner as if he were paid by the minute, 'is that you have been reclassified as a single man. Your tax bill has gone into orbit. It's a fiscal Sputnik.'

'I thought you were supposed to stop that happening.'

'No, *you* have to stop it happening. In the new Germany, the individual takes over more responsibility for his individual destiny. The collectivist Germany is dead. Almost.'

'So what's your role then, Ingo?'

'To help you understand the law. By the way, did Becky leave you any of the tapestries? I remember there was a rather fine Gobelin?'

'Everything went with her to the archaeologist's love nest.'

'Sad. You could have sold off something to pay for your father.'

'She left me with nothing apart from Mac.'

'Well, that can't be all bad. Women impoverish, dogs enrich.'

'I don't think you can make a universal principle out of that.'

'No, you're right. In fact, I'm thinking of a way out of your predicament that involves focussing on the innate wealth of womanhood.' Ingo talked like this when he was embarrassed; in big, rotund sentences that sounded as if they had been translated from Latin.

'Do you mean, find a rich lover?' I studied my frayed cuffs, my stained corduroy trousers that now smelled of Rasputin. 'To be honest, I don't really think I'm gigolo material.'

'Goodness, no,' said Ingo, 'no, no, no – we don't want you selling your body. Or even body parts. Even if you sold a kidney,' Ingo clicked onto Google, 'you would be lucky to fetch €5,000, and that, quite frankly, wouldn't really solve anything at all. Apart from being illegal, I mean. What I had in mind was you selling your soul.'

I stared aghast at my Faustian accountant.

'Well, perhaps I'm over-dramatising a little. It's simply this: under German law, you cut your tax bill in half if you marry someone. It's called *Ehesplitting*, marriage-splitting. You get taxed on your average joint income. So it would be quite absurd to marry a rich woman – unless she was so fabulously rich that taxes became irrelevant. Germany is run secretly by wealthy widows, you know,' – he ran his fishy eyes across my jacket and egg-specked tie – 'but I don't see you as widow-fodder.'

This was getting a bit too intrusive.

'Am I being a bit dim here? You want me to get married to sort out my tax bill?'

'Let's say, it's my very strong recommendation. I'm not saying you should get married for money. On the contrary, the poorer your spouse, the lower your joint taxes. Don't make such a ridiculous expression. Marriage is a contract, who cares about the motivation? One third of all marriages in Germany end in divorce – and do you know which third it is? The 33.33 per cent of couples who were foolish enough to marry for love.'

'It stinks, Ingo.'

'No, marriage is a modern convenience, no more and no less. Remember Jane Austen: "A single man in possession of a good fortune..."'

'It's immoral,' I said and drew back the chair. It was time to leave. I had come to his Dresden chambers expecting hard-nosed advice about investing in Mutual Funds and pork-belly futures and ended up being told that my only market capital was to shed my status as a single man. 'I've been married, it meant something, it ended and it hurt. If I'm going to do it again, it at least has to be an act of free will and not something to please the Inland Revenue.'

'Marriage is like being in the army – everybody complains but you would be surprised at how many people re-enlist. Don't worry, I'll draw up the contracts.'

'Contracts made under duress are invalid.'

'No one is pointing a gun at you.'

'It's a basic violation of morality.'

'I never thought I would hear a journalist use a phrase like that,' said the custodian of my finances. I flinched. 'What's immoral about this? Find a woman whom you like, whom you can live with and who is in a similar situation to yourself. Someone who can make you happy. Preferably someone who likes dogs. Tell her the truth. Sign the deal. What's immoral about that? Immorality only comes into play if you have children. They have the right to know about the foundation of the relationship between father and mother – they have a right to a childhood grounded in truth. But this is a problem that can be solved over time, with care and intelligence. So you see: we can have a conversation about marriage, you and I, without once mentioning the word "love". Love is optional; taxes are not.'

Where Ingo had developed his ideas on marriage, love and parenthood, I don't know. His father loved his golden Retrievers more than he loved his wife, more than Ingo, more even than the Land Rover which he used to transport himself to the weekend hunt. Ingo's father was prepared to send his son to an English boarding school at the age of eight, exchanged perhaps six sentences a week with his wife, but wouldn't be parted from his two hunting dogs, Max and Mum, who would snore and fart in front of the coal fire at the von Landauer castle. Ingo was not an expert on happy families.

I stood up and rather stiffly offered my hand. Then, remembering where his hand had recently been, let it drop.

'Ingo, thank you for everything. It's all a bit too much for me to take on board right now. I'm more or less happy at the moment. I don't need an emotional counsellor. I need cash.'

Ingo unfolded his lanky frame. 'I don't think you understand. You have responsibilities now. You have a child to look after – your father. What is more immoral: to let him die in poverty or to make a tax-friendly marital alliance that could one day open up the possibility of love?'

Chapter Four

England Expects...

'Marriage, eh?' said Harry, staring up at the onion-spired church of St Teresa the Unforgivable. A well-fed priest was waddling like a duck through the graveyard, a bumpy meadow stuffed full of unfortunate mountain climbers, 103-year-old yoghurt-eating locals and soldiers whose bodies had been rescued from some distant war cemetery.

'I can't see it. You, walking up the aisle just to please the Inland Revenue.' On the way down to Bavaria I had informed Harry about my dilemma. He snorted with contempt.

'Look, Harry,' I said sternly, 'it's not about bridesmaids and confetti, it's about raising money to save my poor old dad.'

'Like saving the whales, you mean?' Harry could not hide his dismay. 'Why don't you get Greenpeace involved?'

Before we had a chance to develop this depressing conversation, the priest came within hailing distance. He raised his hand, apparently with great effort and called out: *'Grüss Gott!'* Greetings be to God!

We had come to the village of Oberkrumpet to find an old man who had once served Hitler as a waiter in the Munich restaurant, Osteria Bavaria. Our newspapers had got wind of the possibility that Hitler might not, after all, have been a vegetarian. If the Führer was a carnivore, history would have to be re-written. And the waiter held the key.

The priest, we felt sure, knew the exact address of the veteran waiter. Not that there were many possibilities.

Oberkrumpet was one of those unfortunate Alpine villages positioned on the wrong side of a mountain. Its sister village, Unterkrumpet, caught the sun and was within easy reach of the slopes. Even in the late summer, in the limbo between the hiking and the skiing seasons, it was brimming with life. Teenagers flirted in the village square, gay ski instructors with perfect teeth were having their bodies and their skis waxed in preparation for the first nursery-slope students.

In Oberkrumpet, by contrast, there was a sullen gloom. The sun squeezed through two mountain peaks for about twenty minutes a day. The rest of the time Oberkrumpet seemed to be submerged in dish water. The liveliest spot in town was the cemetery. The youngest villager, we learned later, was a thirteen-year-old boy: the illegitimate offspring of the priest and his housekeeper.

It was, in short, a typical Upper Bavarian community, condemned by the lurking darkness rather than enriched by the life-enhancing qualities of the nearby mountain, the Krumpetspitz.

'That will be Sepp Hanselmeier, you'll be wanting,' said the priest after our lengthy explanation.

We had tried to set out our mission without once mentioning Hitler. No point in further scaring a village which was already frightened of its own shadow. We knew very little of Hanselmeier: only that he had become a ship's cook during the war. Afterwards he had made French fries for American soldiers.

The priest's instructions were precise: down the high street, past the baker's and the pub and then a sharp right until we reached a house where all the shutters would be closed. The priest did not mention that it would also be the place where a silver Mercedes Cabrio would be parked, roof rolled down so we could admire the cappuccino-coloured leather seats.

'The Führer must have tipped well,' grumbled Harry when he saw the car.

'God, it looks so depressing,' I said, taking in the crumbling, carved wooden balustrades, the brownness of it all.

'Just as well we didn't bring Tony,' said Harry. 'We would have ended up slitting our wrists.'

Tony was in the midst of a week-long argument with his wife and had withdrawn from our trip at the last moment. His Ibsen-like melancholy was not what I needed. Von Landauer's interpretation of filial duty and his analysis of my finances had already plunged me into a black hole. Only Harry's relentless cheerleading was keeping me afloat. And even that was a little suspect.

'I mean, let's face it, look at yourself,' he said, pressing the bell marked Hanselmeier and still chewing on my marriage prospects. 'Who would look at you?'

As if on one cue, the door was flung open by a rigorously coiffeured woman with arched eyebrows, a beaked nose and thin lips. Her hair was so tightly curled it could have opened a wine bottle. She was expensively dressed, in a designer version of a dirndl, and surrounded by a cloud of Chloé perfume. This had been Becky's favourite scent and I reacted like a behaviourally conditioned laboratory rat, suddenly perky and sexually awake. She, however, ignored me.

'*Grüss Gott*. What can I do for you?'

'We're here to see your father,' I blurted out. 'We're the journalists who rang from Berlin.'

'Grandfather,' corrected Harry, 'your grandfather. Is that your car out there? Beautiful model.' He looked the woman up and down.

Frau Hanselmeier reached out a hand with red talons. A platinum charm bracelet slid forward, over the wristbone. Harry held the hand for a little too long and stared deeply into her eyes. Frau Hanselmeier did not look once at me. 'Why don't you come in and we can talk.'

Her dirndl swung as we followed her into the gabled low-ceilinged living room. It was the usual Bavarian jumble of antlers and stuffed ferrets and mismatched Meissen and glass bookshelves creaking with unread subscription-only encyclopedias.

'She's a bit of all right,' whispered Harry as if he were a theatre prompter. 'Forty years old and as crisp as a piece of pork crackling.'

'Thirty-eight actually,' said Frau Hanselmeier in perfect English. She turned her glacial gaze on Harry.

'Take a seat,' she said pointing to a dinner table with a vase of dried summer flowers. 'Could I see your cards?' She screwed up her eyes to read Harry's, which read in big script: 'THE DAILY TORMENT', and then in somewhat smaller letters, 'HARRY BALL', and then microscopically, 'correspondent for special projects'.

'So my grandfather,' she threw a withering, dominatrix-type glance in my direction, 'has become a "special project". I would like you both to know that I'm a lawyer,' she handed out embossed cards from a Munich legal office, 'and I'm dedicated to protecting the privacy of my grandfather. With all possible means.'

'Look, dear,' said Harry, deciding he had established enough intimacy, 'we're not trying to track down a war criminal. Just curious about how it was to serve food to Hitler.'

'And why should that be of any interest to anyone?'

I launched into a nervous discourse about how food and Nazism was now the new hot area of British historical research. Did eating cabbage make the Germans fight harder? Or merely smell different?

'Your father, er, grandfather, could help us solve the last riddle of the Third Reich,' I said, swept up with the excitement of the mission. 'What did Hitler really eat?'

Frau Hanselmeier sat silent for a while. Somewhere inside the room we could hear the impatient buzz of the last of the summer wasps. Harry and I exchanged glances. Where was our waiter?

'So you want to make my grandfather, my old, crippled grandfather, into an icon for right-wing extremists? To show them that Hitler was a True German right down to his intestines? Maybe the Allies concocted the story that he was a vegetarian to make him seem like a wimp?'

Frau Hanselmeier was flaring up now, her eyes ablaze at the imagined wrong. Her breast heaved inside – but only just – her light, white blouse.

'We will have Neo-Nazis knocking on our door day and night. They will make him into the new Rudolf Hess! Where will it end? Perhaps television will make a film series about Hitler's sausages! The shame of it all!'

We sat open-mouthed at this operatic performance. Bavarian lawyers were clearly passionate creatures.

'No, no,' said Harry, turning his brown eyes on Frau Hanselmeier, 'we are not going to sell your grandfather to Nazi souvenir hunters. We just think you are what you eat.'

'Or that what you eat says something about your life-philosophy,' I chipped in.

'And what you don't eat tells you a lot too. Historically speaking.'

We were getting very confused.

'My grandfather is an old man, he needs protection. Perhaps,' Frau Hanselmeier choked back a simulated sob, 'he doesn't have much time to live.'

Harry nodded sagely. 'All the more reason to get his impressions written down now, for the history books, so to speak.'

'All the more reason, I think, to pay him,' said Frau Hanselmeier. From underneath the table she hoisted up a brown leather satchel and withdrew two pieces of paper. 'I would feel happier if we had this in writing.'

She pushed the sheets over the varnished surface. One guaranteed Sepp Hanselmeier his privacy rights, the other was an agreement to pay two-thousand euros for the interview.

'Can't pay you, I'm afraid, Frau Hanselmeier,' I said after reading the text. 'It's against our code of ethics.'

'Ethics?' expostulated the Bavarian lawyer. 'We have a product, and we live in a free market.'

'Ethics?' asked Harry, puzzled by the word.

'Ethics,' I said with a little less certainty. My newspaper, I knew, had no problems with spending large sums for the dubious memoirs of footballers. The ethical boundaries were fluid. But they were almost certainly opposed to paying Hitler's waiter.

'Perhaps we could talk about this in a different room,' said Harry. Frau Hanselmeier stood up, so did Harry. 'Not you!' he hissed, as I drew back my chair. I heard the wooden creak of the stairs as they went upstairs to continue the negotiation.

Left alone, I wandered round the room, picking up dusty pieces of porcelain, an old pewter beer mug, a well-thumbed maritime history of the world.

The page fell open at naval battles. Sepp was plainly still a man of the sea.

The account of the Battle of Trafalgar provided some kind of inspiration. Before sending his ships into battle Nelson ordered a signal to be sent – by hoisting the coded flags – to the British warships: 'England expects that every man will do his duty.'

We had learned the line in school but I had long since forgotten it. All that British schoolchildren remembered now about Nelson was that, while dying, he told an officer to kiss him, suggesting a modern bisexuality. But the British of my generation had a sense of duty that was every bit as developed and as strict as the Prussian. There was nothing specifically Prussian about dying for one's country, obeying orders or struggling to do the right thing. And there was the heart of the matter: I had a responsibility, an old-fashioned duty, towards my father, that demanded sacrifice. England expects...

I read further. After Nelson was killed by a French sniper during the battle, his men put his body in a cask of rum to preserve it during the long journey home. The barrel was full when the ship set out; by the time the ship arrived in England, the barrel was half empty. Sailors had been secretly tapping the barrel for mugs of rum, despite its pickled contents. There were many ways, it seemed, for an Englishman to do his duty. One was the Harry way.

At last he and Frau Hanselmeier burst into the room, both smiling beatifically as if they had just bathed in molten chocolate or taken serotonin-boosters.

'Right, sorted that out,' said Harry, adjusting his trouser belt and clasping his hands on his knees.

'Indeed we did,' said Frau Hanselmeier. 'I don't think we will be needing these.' She ripped up the contracts.

'What the hell did you do?' I whispered to Harry.

'Professional secret,' he said. 'The least said about it the better.' He tapped the side of his nose.

'I shall fetch my grandfather,' said Frau Hanselmeier who seemed to have lost her bitterness. Suddenly the hardened lawyer had become as soft as fresh whitebread. She even smelled differently, the Chloé having given way to something more salty.

'*Das schönste Blümlein auf der Alm,*' came a strong but croaking voice, reminiscent of Rod Stewart on amphetamines. Or off amphetamines. *The most beautiful little flower on the slopes.*

'*Das ist das Edelweiss.*' That is the Edelweiss. It was Sepp Hanselmeier wheeled into the room by his strangely liberated granddaughter. Sepp was obviously determined to finish the song. He was also equally obviously very drunk indeed.

'*Es blüht versteckt auf steiler Höh.*' Sepp, his face as yellow as parchment, began to wave his arms. In his imagination perhaps he was in the Hofbräuhaus, stirring up his neighbours before the white sausage arrived.

'*So zwischen Schnee und Eis…*'

'That's enough, Granddad,' said Frau Hanselmeier. 'Now you're going to answer the questions of these nice men.' She winked at Harry. 'I'll leave you to it, gentlemen. If he gets too much for you, shout, and I'll be back.'

'Good girl,' hiccupped Sepp. 'Used to be a wild one.' I glanced at Harry whose face did not flicker. 'Has she gone yet?' He looked over his shoulder. 'Good.'

Sepp stepped nimbly out of his wheelchair, he swayed slightly but it was the gait of an old sailor rather than of a man with ill legs. He walked over to the bookcase and reached behind the naval history book to bring out a bottle of Jägermeister.

'Sorry about the wheelchair.' He shrugged, setting out three glasses. 'The bloody rules about disability pensions have become so tough. They're checking all the time. Couldn't be sure you weren't snoopers from some agency. What do you want to know?'

Slowly, drink by drink, we were given a picture of the pubs and restaurants of pre-war Munich. It was a time of big eating, big drinking and big tips. Sepp had been no more than a junior apprentice waiter, the bottom of the hierarchy. 'The cook would slap me if I wasn't quick enough, or if he thought I was letting the food get cold. Then the senior waiter would hit me, and then the other waiters. Some customers would even hit me. It was good preparation for the war.'

Hitler was a regular, a very precise eater. There were no obvious signs that he was a vegetarian because there was no such thing as a potato soup without a chunk of ham or a green bean soup without some floating bacon. So perhaps Hitler ate the vegetables and left the meat.

'Do you know the phrase *Hundekurve*, the "dog curve"? No, of course not. You have probably never got your feet wet.' Sepp was, however, ensuring that our throats were wet. We were, by the time he had reached Hitler's eating habits, well into our second bottle of Jägermeister, a detergent-like medicinal Schnapps.

'You know how a dog will chase a sausage tied to a string, in a long curve. During the war I became a ship's cook in a Torpedo boat and that's what we used to call our tactics, sweeping alongside the British warships.'

We nodded, gradually worn down by an old man's ramblings and by the alcohol.

'Well, that's what it was like when we served Hitler. He couldn't stand anyone approaching him from behind, and he was upset by the sight of a waiter in front of him. We had to make a *Hundekurve* with our mineral water, our herbal tea, our cheese cake...

'As for meat...' Sepp's voice tapered off. We waited patiently for the narrative to resume. Harry got ready to switch on the tape recorder. We were about to get what we had come for.

Instead there was silence.

'Sepp?'

'Herr Hanselmeier?'

'Oh, shit.' The old man's head had slumped to his chest.

'Is he dead?'

'How can he die before spilling his last secret?'

'His *only* secret.'

'Herr Hanselmeier.' Harry shook the old man.

'Perhaps we should call for his granddaughter.'

'Are you mad? She'll accuse us of killing him.'

'Try mouth-to-mouth.' Harry, as usual, had taken charge of the situation by issuing orders.

'Have you smelled him?'

'Could be a matter of life and death.'

'So you try it.'

I reached over, squeezed his hairy nostril closed and started to breathe into his mouth, in an unpleasantly intimate gesture, half remembered from school first-aid classes.

'Don't be a fool, he should be laid down.'

We pulled Sepp off the chair and lay him on the floor.

'Do you put a pillow under his feet or not?'

'Can't remember.'

Harry was not being helpful. I tried again to revive Sepp. Nostril closed. Breathe in. Breathe out.

'I can't hear his heart,' said Harry.

'That's because you're two metres away,' I said, gulping in some air.

'It's probably his heart, that's what we should be pumping.'

I started to breathe again into the old man's mouth.

Suddenly he sat up, like a deckchair abruptly unfolded. He took one look at me and slapped me hard, as hard, I am sure, as he was hit in the Osteria Bavaria.

'Don't touch me, you pervert,' he shouted. 'You bloody English are all the same. I know your type from the Navy.'

Then he fell back and started to snore loudly.

'Well, he seems to be alive,' said Harry, not quite as relieved as he should have been.

'Yes,' I said, rubbing my face.

'What about the story?' said Harry.

'Let's give it up, I've had enough.'

'Don't be ridiculous. You don't know what I've already done for this interview.'

'What do you mean?'

'Never you mind. Let's have a quick look round.'

He started to open drawers.

'What are you doing?'

'For God's sake man, no time for your absurd principles. Sepp was a sailor and sailors always have hiding places. That's the way it is when you're living up close.'

'What are we looking for?'

'Don't know, something that connects him with Hitler's stomach. He wouldn't have thrown that away.'

I started to look in the bookshelves where the Jägermeister had been stashed.

'Nothing here, just bills,' said Harry, rifling through the drawers. 'And a secret hoard of tobacco. I bet Gertrud doesn't let him smoke.'

Gertrud?

'Harry,' I said, 'did you...?' Then I remembered the bookmark in the Great Naval Battles book and pulled the volume off the shelf.

'I think we've got something.'

It was a menu from the Osteria Bavaria. *'Petite Poussin'* — spring chicken. In the corner, someone had written: 'Thank you for such splendid service, A.H.'

'Typical Hitler,' said Harry, 'probably signed the menu rather than give a tip. Mean bastard.'

'Dictators, eh? Don't you just love them?'

Harry took a photograph of the menu and we placed it carefully back in the book. Sepp's last secret returned to its proper place between the Battles of Skagerrak and Dogger Bank.

Harry looked down at the prone figure of the drunken sailor and shook his head: 'Whatever happened to German discipline? They've let themselves go.'

Chapter Five

More Haste, Less Speed

There was nothing very Prussian about the Preussen-Eck, even if the pub was named after the defunct state.

The faded tablecloths were punctuated by burn- or perhaps bullet-holes; plastic flowers, paper napkins, the heavy odour of cheap tobacco clung to the curtains and, as the door of the toilets swung open and closed, customers were treated to concentrated gusts of male urine. It was like a prison visiting room, without the reinforced glass shields.

On the first Monday of every month the pub held a jazz evening for Berliners whose idea of pleasure was to listen to scratchy Duke Ellington. And on Saturdays it was local Berlin soccer fans, stopping by for a beer or three after losing their latest game.

It wasn't much of a financial proposition for a pub so it was no surprise that the owner should rent out the ballroom for speed-dating, the strange, modern version of mating for men and women who did not want to waste time being charming.

I could not believe I was here, standing at the bar filling in a form that, together with my twenty-euro entrance fee, was supposed to put me on the route to a financially advantageous marriage.

On the road back from Oberkrumpet, I had asked Harry about his encounter with Frau Hanselmeier.

She had been quietly philosophical about comatose Sepp. There was after all a long naval tradition of preserving people in alcohol. If Sepp's liver did not give up, a state of perpetual marination would keep him as Hitler's gastronomic witness for years to come.

We could only hope that one of Germany's Nazi-tainment TV producers would not discover him for a new spurious series on Hitler's digestive organs.

Frau Hanselmeier had slapped her grandfather round a bit and then, together with Harry, taken him upstairs to bed. Harry had stayed with her for a while apparently conducting another round of negotiations.

'Sometimes these things happen really quickly. It knocks you for six,' said Harry, taking in my astonishment at how rapidly he had broken down Gertrud Hanselmeier's defences.

'Chemistry,' I mused, though I had never quite believed in it. And failed the subject in school.

'No, more physics and biology.'

'What about history? Geography?' I was baffled. Nothing had ever gone swiftly for me.

'Speed is the one genuinely modern pleasure,' said Harry and to make the point pushed his smart brown brogue shoe on the peddle, overtaking another Mercedes dawdling along at 160 kmph.

We drove in silence for a while. Then Harry slapped the steering wheel.

'Of course, that's it! Speed dating! That's what you should do! No money squandered on expensive dinners, no brain-numbing small talk.'

'Stupid idea. It'll be like having a candlelit McDonalds.'

'It's time you understood – this is not about romance. You have to sort out your finances, just think about your poor dad. Use every legal mechanism. That includes marriage. *Basta!*' Harry had evidently changed his mind about marriage as a solution. It must have been the mountain air. 'First you have to establish your market value. There might be women out there absolutely gagging for you. Strange place, Berlin.'

And so, with trepidation, to the Preussen-Eck.

What kind of market was this? I pondered in the run-down pub, surveying the field. A cattle market, perhaps.

We were seven men, connected only by our desperation and determination to meet as many women as cheaply and as quickly as possible.

There was a hairy, oafish man, swathed in muscle that had turned into fat, squeezed into a C&A shirt.

Twins in their late twenties, studying mechanical engineering, a teacher with a woolly beard and an earring, a ticket inspector with a pierced nose and an army major.

Spread out across the table were a sheaf of forms. Speed dating might be an Anglo-Saxon invention but it had to conform to the German sense of order.

The procedure was that seven women would sit at seven tables. The men would make an attempt to capture their attention for seven minutes and then move onto the next table.

First, however, both men and women had to fill in forms which were as long and as dense and as unanswerable as the citizenship tests handed out to would-be Germans. Instead of being asked the names of three mountains or the composer of the Ninth Symphony, we were required to answer questions like 'Do you believe in God?' and 'When did your last relationship end?'

'Do we believe in God?' asked one twin.

'Not since Mum was robbed in the street,' said his brother.

'So shall we say "no"?' The dominant twin wrinkled his brow.

'You can say "yes", I'll say "no", then if one of us gets a Christian, we can swap. She'll never tell the difference.'

The rest of us looked on bemused.

'This question is a disgrace,' said the big man. '"How much do you earn?" The women will obviously choose the richest man.' He scanned the competition to assess who could possibly be richer than him. I saw the teacher write 'Audi Quattro – red' next to the question 'What car do you have?'

'Teaching is paying better than it used to, I see.'

The teacher sensed scepticism in my voice.

'I have independent means.'

'Ah,' I said, 'after-hours tuition, eh?'

The army officer, fit but greying at the temples, filled out his form first.

'I have only one question remaining,' he boomed. 'Where are the women?'

It was a legitimate enquiry.

Gisela, the mistress of ceremonies, appeared at our side. She wore a smart blue blazer and a white pleated skirt. Her face resembled that of an English police sergeant. Not a woman to be crossed.

'The ladies,' she said, stressing *ladies*, 'are completing their forms round the corner. The procedure is as follows: when the ladies are seated — and not a second before! — you will approach a table and exchange forms. You will proceed to have spontaneous conversation until I sound the gong.'

She pointed to the kind of metal disc you see gathering dust in Chinese restaurants.

'Then you will tick the boxes provided. "Yes" — meaning you want me to pass on your e-mail address, "no" — meaning you never want to see this woman again, and "friendship" — meaning you are willing to begin a sexless relationship. Now, is that clear?'

Even the testosterone-driven major seemed cowed by this dominatrix.

One by one, the women filed to the tables. There was a red-haired beauty with pale freckled complexion and high cheekbones, a giantess who looked like a basketball player, a dumpy but clever-looking woman in denims. The other four entered the room so quickly it was impossible to assess their appearance or their manner. One, bizarrely, wore sunglasses. Even on jazz night, nobody wore sunglasses in the Preussen-Eck.

'Gentlemen, you may take your places,' said Gisela, with the firm tone of a referee in a boxing match calling on the fighters to leave their corners.

I had dreaded this moment and cursed Harry for nudging me into this situation. It reminded me of school dances.

Once every three months girls from the local convent school would be bussed over. In a great Chernobyl-like cloud of cheap perfume they would be lined up on the far side of the gym. We were allowed, as a special privilege, to wear ordinary clothes rather than school uniform.

For weeks we had taken dance classes, for hours we had gossiped after lights-out until the dawn, speculating about who we would end up with. We purged our breath with Odol, sprayed our armpits with Rexona, squeezed blackheads and prepared ourselves for battle.

But we did not know what to say.

The older kids gave us tips. Earwax, they said, could be cleaned out by soaking a cloth with paraffin and then lighting it. Sometimes the advice was flawed, or missing a critical component, but it was always recited with masculine certainty, as part of a folk wisdom that had been passed down from great uncles or long dead but unimpeachably successful ancestors.

Yet no one taught us how to talk to women or, worse still, teenage girls with social skills as stunted as ourselves. So we would stand and stare until a teacher ordered us to ask a girl to dance. Most of us were pleased when it was all over.

The same sense of helplessness overcame me as I sat down at table one. We had all been given a glass of prosecco to loosen our tongues. I put my form down next to the woman's and quickly read the first details – twenty-six, Rhinelander,

Catholic, cat owner, ambition to meet a boy band – before looking up at her face. It was pleasant: hovis-skinned, teeth like a chipmunk, an honest smile.

'Janine,' she said, holding out her hand and tumbling her glass of Prosecco over my form.

'Oh God, I'm so sorry. Now I won't know who you are.'

'It's OK,' I said, through gritted teeth. 'There are photocopies. Let's just talk about you.'

'I'm boring, really,' she said. Already I sensed this was not false modesty.

'I'm sure that isn't true. You say your favourite writer is Rosamund Pilcher.'

'Well, I watch her on TV on Sundays. Do you?'

'No, I watch *Tales of the Unknown.*'

'Are you from Cornwall? It looks so romantic on TV.'

'Been there once. Very cold. They don't have central heating.'

'Is it true that the English sleep with their bedroom windows open?'

'Don't the Germans?'

'No.'

'What do you do, er, Janine?'

'I'm a business woman.'

'Really? What line of business?'

'Retail.'

'So you work in a shop?'

'Yes. A delicatessen.'

'In the meat department?'

'Yes. How did you know?'

'Your hands are full of little scratches. From slicing.'

She looked down at her hands and started to cry.

'I didn't mean it personally. I just notice these things.'

Janine was inconsolable. She sobbed and sobbed. All the other tables stared at me. They had me down as a misogynist, capable of destroying a woman in – what? – six minutes, twelve seconds.

'Look, Janine, I'm sorry. You've got very nice hands.'

'Don't you touch me!' She was shouting now. 'You're as bad as my father, the bastard, always interfering with me, he was! No wonder my mother killed herself. The poor, poor woman.'

Janine was now head in hands, shaking with a deep misery that had somehow un-bottled.

Six minutes, forty seconds.

'Get out of my sight, go on!'

The gong sounded. B-o-n-g.

'Sorry, Janine,' I said rather lamely, 'will you be all right?'

Gisela the ringmaster was already in the centre of the room. 'Now, everyone fill in your forms – yes, no or friendship – and move on one table.'

I turned away from Janine so that she wouldn't see me mark 'no'. Or rather: NO!!!

'Nice meeting you, Janine.'

I could see that speed dating was not exactly the pragmatist's dream I had imagined it to be. When Harry had first mentioned it, I had pictured a kind of postmodern, virtual harem. Instead it was a Darwinian nightmare: men compete, women choose.

The men were all sweating. The Preussen-Eck hadn't been this hot since the days of the postwar economic miracle when pubs deliberately switched up the heating to increase consumption of beer. We had knocked back our proseccos but that alone could not account for the perspiration that was brimming even from the brow of the army man. The other men had it easier than me but they were still shattered by the effort of trying to be attractive for seven concentrated minutes.

'You had quite an effect on that woman,' said the teacher. 'Are you going to break all their hearts?' His face had a naturally sneering look, the tugged facial lines made famous by George Bush junior. I suppose he taught maths.

'I have a cruel side,' I said. The teacher took the words at face value, and shook his head as if to say: this monster will never be successful with women, or in his life.

'Let me give you a tip,' he said, 'women want men who listen to them. Pretend to listen until you have caught them – so!' He raised his hand and snapped it closed as if catching an *Aedes vexans*, the mosquito that had been plaguing the German capital throughout the muggy, damp summer.

'Thank you,' I said, and took my seat at the next table.

It was the woman with sunglasses.

'Blind?' I asked, deciding I would present myself as a uniquely sympathetic male. 'I've always thought blind people were specially privileged.'

'Shall I take off my glasses?'

'Please.'

She had arctic blue eyes. They were the most interesting feature of a sad, narrow face.

'You can see me.' I was not surprised. I had been mocking her. The Preussen-Eck was certainly not the place to play Audrey Hepburn.

'Dust allergy.'

'It's the Sahara sands.'

'You're a journalist?' I nodded and searched for her profession on the form. She had written in a tight, cramped script and I couldn't read most of it without my glasses.

'Are you happy in the job?'

'Yes. No. Not sure.'

'But, you're pretty old, you must know by now.'

She had a point.

'Life's complicated. What do you do?'

'Accountant.'

'Oh, that's good.'

'Finanzamt Wilmersdorf.'

'Oh.' The Finanzamt was the German Inland Revenue. And Wilmersdorf was now my tax zone.

'Do you have a problem with that? Do you have a problem with working women?'

'No, really, no problem. It's great. Women should work more. Er… ' I scrambled to find her name, ' …Bettina. What do you read?'

'Rosamund Pilcher.'

My heart sank.

'Is there a problem with that too?'

'No, no.'

We fell silent. Seven minutes can be a very long time. Round me, my male competitors were doing fine. The twins, at neighbouring tables, were telepathically finishing each other's identical conversation with two bemused female candidates. The major was advancing inch-by-inch as if he was an officer in the Somme in 1915.

'Do you believe in God?' I could hear him reading out from the form.

'No,' said his counterpart, the squat, clever woman in Pepe jeans, 'money.'

'That's good,' he said, 'money can be very spiritual.'

The most successful in the male team was the big hairy oaf in the C&A shirt. I could see his feet under the picnic table touching the calves of the basketball player. It must have been the King Kong effect. Girls fall for gorillas.

My gaze returned to Bettina. We had talked ourselves to a standstill. Suddenly I saw the trace of a bubbling tear rolling down her cheek, gathering pace like a skier.

'Damned allergy,' she said, wiping it away and replacing her dark glasses.

'Yeah, dust everywhere. Bloody Prussians.' Berlin, indeed the whole region of Brandenburg, was built on sand.

The gong sounded. B-o-n-g.

I got up without a word, offered my hand.

'Friends?'

'When I recover my sight. Where do you live by the way?'

I told her that I was moving to Grunewald.

'That's my tax-district.' It sounded like a warning.

The twins, the gorilla, the major and the teacher were in boisterous mood, drinking quickly at the bar before we moved tables. The teacher was bragging.

'So I said to my one – can I buy you a drink? And she said, straight out, OK but I'm not going to sleep with you. What kind of world do we live in? What happened to the middle bit, the gap between bar and bed?'

'Berlin girls,' said King Kong, 'they're animals.'

I looked at my watch. Speed dating was more like slow torture.

Gisela the Ring Master tugged me gently away from the men.

'If you make one more woman cry,' she said with barely concealed menace, 'I will have to ask you to leave. I don't know what you are saying in your seven minutes but I can't accept someone systematically causing emotional crisis in my clients.'

'The last one was a dust allergy,' I protested.

'You will get your money back. I know I shouldn't have let a journalist take part. An *English* journalist. Speed dating is such a sensitive process.'

It was time to move to table three. The woman sitting there, straight-backed as if at a Victorian dinner party, had extraordinary presence. She commanded her corner of the room like a general surveying the line-up of battle.

'Hello,' I said, looking at her form, 'you must be Renata – but you remind me of Napoleon. Prettier, of course. Much prettier.'

'Taller, too,' she said and stood up.

It was the red-headed beauty that I had spotted at the outset of the evening. Her cheekbones were striking, more Norman than Slavic. She looked as if she could be comfortable selling camembert and calvados in a village shop, or running some magnificent but rotting chateau. According to Ingo's logic – or rather the twisted calculations of the German tax laws – it would be better if she were a shopkeeper than a chateau-owner. But for the first time I felt that something might work. Despite Harry's pithy analysis, it wasn't just physics and biology; it felt right.

'Renata, you must promise me this before we start talking – please, don't cry. If you are going to shed tears, then do so in ten minutes. Otherwise I get thrown out.'

'I promise only to yawn if you are boring.'

Renata, it emerged, was a single mother and an unemployed or underemployed sculptress. Her dream was to create the perfect war memorial.

'What does that mean?'

'Something that makes war into more than simple victimhood. I want to show war as a process, not a freak event. Memory's so important, don't you think?'

I hadn't anticipated an intellectual debate in a seven-minute sprint. But it was always refreshing to talk intelligently to an attractive woman; it gave an intensity to thought, an artificial clarity, like drinking meths.

'It's about fighting stupidity rather than preserving memories,' I said.

But before I could dazzle Renata with my insights into war, the mobile phone rang.

'Son, can you talk?'

'Not really, can you call me in exactly three minutes, twenty seconds?'

'No, son, this is too important. The bailiffs have moved in. They're taking away my piano! Our piano!'

'My God!' I mimed to Renata that I had to deal with a crisis. Renata cast me a strange glance, picked at her ringless fingers.

The piano had been the centrepiece of our family. It was nothing special, the kind of rough, battered instrument one saw in saloon bars or brothels in cowboy films. But it was always in use: on Saturdays after Dad came back from the pub, on birthdays, at Christmas. Britain used to be a piano-playing country. Songs like 'Heart of Oak' and 'Boney Was A Warrior' were the patriotic pulse of our society, songs that told of bravery, strong decisions, hatred of the French and a long-lost Empire. The piano was the connection between the chauvinism of the 1890s, World War Two and the troubled identity of the postwar years.

For Dad, it was even more. In the war, pilots used to let off steam by hammering the keys. It was, I think, a time of frenzied dancing and of brief but very intense romances. Dancing, in those days, meant sex rather than self-display as it does today. Dad had wanted to bring part of his single-man's biography into the family home with his piano. That, and a few books, was all that he brought to the marriage. The rest: the furniture, the drapes, the porcelain and the cutlery came from my mother. So we would sing round the piano but only when my father played. Then it was special and mysterious, though not, admittedly, very competent.

Now the piano was being manhandled out of the house. I could picture the scene: two sweating, heavy-duty movers with slings, cursing as they negotiated their way down the narrow stairs.

'That's awful, Dad. How do you feel?'

'How do you think I feel?' It was said with anger rather than self-pity. My father's life was being dismantled.

'I've got to talk to you, Dad.'

'We're talking, aren't we?'

'No, I mean face to face.'

'I don't want to see anyone at the moment. I'm not fit for human contact.'

'Wait a second.'

The gong had just rung out, this time with a terrifyingly loud resonance as in a Buddhist temple.

'That will be your dinner bell,' said my father, 'you had better be going.'

'No, hang on… ' I turned to Renata and hissed 'TICK MY BOX!' She smiled enigmatically and then quite inexplicably started to cry.

'That's it!' said Gisela, advancing on me like a gendarme. 'I warned you – leave now! At this very moment!'

'Renata?' I gasped, baffled by my bad luck. But Renata had covered her face with her hands. What was going on? What had I said? Then, I remembered the phone.

'Dad?' My father had hung up.

Outside, it had begun to rain. A mosquito settled on my moist arm. It sat there as if considering whether to dine now or later. I swatted it, missed and hit my watch strap instead. It broke.

Chapter Six

A Change of Address

The letter took me by surprise. It was the first one addressed to my new apartment and the first one from my father that was not linked to a formal anniversary. The handwriting on the envelope was careful, even elegant, as if written with great concentration.

I remembered faking his signature on medical excuse chits. *Unfortunately my son has been struggling with a bad bout of rheumatic fever during the holidays and his doctor advises that he should not play sport for the first three weeks of term.*

I used the same forgery – changing only the date – for three autumn terms in a row and was thus spared the first cross-country runs of the season, the breathless, pointless trudge through the English mud.

So I knew every curl and twist of his vowels and consonants, the jagged Y, the squashed O that always looked like a pumpkin.

The handwriting had become more spidery over the years but it was still unmistakably the script of a man who wrote rarely, but not idly: with firm intent.

It was the day of the move. We had collected a rental van from Robben and Wientjes on the previous evening and loaded it up.

Harry was there, so was Tony and my office intern, Jonathan, who was willing to put up with any amount of unpaid humiliation in return for a generous reference. Together we had packed the Ikea wardrobe and the Billy shelves into cardboard boxes donated by the local supermarket's fruit-and-veg department.

I slept the night on the floor, travelled with my team to Grunewald, opened the door, gave my orders, emptied the postbox and made my way back by S-Bahn, Berlin's overground railway, to Prenzlauer Berg to hand over the old, vacated apartment to the landlord.

How many times had I performed this operation in the past? Six, seven times? It should have been an emotionally wrenching experience but over time I came to regard it as routinely as surgeon performing a hernia op; moving house for an Englishman was almost a reflex action. For Germans, I sensed, it was something far more traumatic. The mere act of shifting furniture seemed to evoke troubled times; bombed-out homes, families on the run.

The S-Bahn was full of people leaning their drained faces against the window, clutching over-priced coffee in take-away polystyrene cups. An unwashed homeless man tried to sell me a newspaper. Since I was also unwashed and between homes I should have felt some solidarity but was too preoccupied to look for a euro.

Opposite me sat a man dressed with suspicious precision in a woven tie, and cufflinks that flashed from a flannel jacket. Only his curling, frayed shirt collar suggested that not all was well. He smiled at the woman sitting next to him. She immediately sought a place somewhere else.

Then he turned his wide, happy, charming grin at me: *'Bessa als die Nervenanstalt, wah?' Better here than in the clinic, isn't it?*

'Yes,' I said doubtfully, 'a bit better,' and gathered my courage to open the envelope.

Dear Son,

I hadn't expected to write you this letter. You have your life, I have mine. I haven't always approved of your lifestyle, you know that. True Englishmen should find ways of serving their country, wherever they are, otherwise what's left? What's the point of fighting tyranny abroad if you don't stay at home to fight for what you believe in there?

I sighed. Was this going to be a rant against immigration? It saddened me that my father, who I knew to be a decent and relatively open man, should have ranted like a National Front huckster whenever life was a bit difficult.

I looked up. The happy Berliner madman was still staring at me. I looked down again.

If only you had taken a decent job in the office of a decent British company, you would better understand what we're all facing here in Britain.

Dad, having accepted that I would never be a soldier or a pilot, entertained a fantasy that I could become a rich and influential industrialist. His uncle Rufus was in the Yorkshire wool business and I had spent an excruciatingly boring summer holiday learning about office life in his factory.

In the office at the mill I learned about the Italian Jacket system. You kept a spare jacket in the office. To steal time from your boss, you spread this jacket over the back of the chair to give the impression that you had only briefly left your place, for a vital conference. The practise had been imported from Italy, where there are always more attractive alternatives to work.

Wearing your proper jacket, you slipped out of the clatter of the air-conditioned office into the real world for a couple of hours. It was enough to go to a nearby park and feed the ducks in the sunshine to reclaim a sense of individuality. The mill, naturally, went bankrupt. Later though, I introduced the Italian Jacket to my newspaper colleagues and they took to it like liberated slaves. One used his jacket as an alibi for an out-of-office romance, escaping for three hours a day. Another would disappear for a Thai massage. There was something deeply satisfying about cheating your boss – and demonstrating to yourself and to your colleagues that you could work in a perfectly competent way without being constantly present.

Through spies or the rat-like cunning of the managerial class, the editor was made aware of the fact that I was the moving spirit behind something subversive. The time had come, he decided, to banish me from the office world and indeed from England.

And so I became a foreign correspondent, a professional exile. It was the end of my life as an office saboteur, but my father still thought of me as someone who had turned his back on England and on honest working life.

Things are going to the dogs here, continued my father's epistle. *The prime minister is a fool, the opposition are numbskulls, we're being run by traitors who are plotting to bring down our country.*

The out-patient from the Berlin psychiatric clinic was still smiling at me. I smiled back. Passengers started to move away from me too.

They are determined to deny our history, to "Europeanise" it, make us into one big Brussels blancmange in which there are no battles, no defeats and no grudges. Everything has just become an orgy of pointless reconciliation. I'm fed up with it. Now they're going for me! I wrote to the prime minister to tell him he was betraying Britain by considering joining the euro. No reply, of course! What do you expect from a man who puts his hand in his pocket when he makes speeches. Completely lacking in respect.

I sighed. There was so much anger stored in my father. Could you inherit anger? Did I have an anger gene?

The latest development: somebody's been trying to get into the house. As if the financial problems weren't enough! The lock on the backdoor has been tampered with. The other day I went to the pub to meet Tom. When I came back, two windows were wide open. You know me, I never open windows — fresh air kills, we were always agreed on that, if nothing else. Tom is sure that the secret services have been put on my case since I wrote to the prime minister. They think I know something.'

Tom was a wartime friend of my father's and a profoundly bad influence. Long years in journalism had taught me to take persecution complexes seriously: paranoia was to be in possession of all the facts. But Tom had a knack of stirring trouble. He was an embittered man and there is nothing more dangerous than a bitter friend. My father, I had known for years, was slightly crazy. He was, however, benignly mad, in a state of gentle confusion. Tom's poisonous utterances gave a nasty edge to my father's ramblings.

They're after me, son, they're after all of us old heroes, because we're the ones who can remember. That's why they're pulling apart my existence...

The letter meandered on. The happy passenger had got off at the Chancellery. Nobody was smiling any more.

Tom and I have decided it's time to show our faces in Germany again. You know my view has always been: east is east, west is west and ne'er the twain shall meet. I've got really nothing to say to the Huns and they've got nothing to say to us. But Tom's sort of persuaded me: we're heroes because Germans remember what we did, even if they don't like us for it. They know a thousand times more than our young generation does. Tom says they've got a memory muscle that gets exercised all their lives.

Outside, Berlin flashed by. We had crossed what used to be no-mans-land between West and East Berlin. Soon I would have to change trains. Where was my father? In no-mans-land? About to change the views of a lifetime?

There's a reunion at some airbase in the Rhineland, continued the letter. '*The Germans are paying for everything so you don't have to worry about that. I'll even save a bit. Won't have to buy my own food for a few days!*

Was that the real reason for my father's impending visit? Travelling to Germany, still obscurely regarded as the enemy, could be seen as an act of desperation: not some half-baked attempt at reconciliation but a way of getting food in his stomach and keeping his feet warm.

The next sentence suggested that the trip was part of a mutual guilt game, a Freudian *pas de deux* that had been going on since I was a child.

Sounds strange, but I'm looking forward to eating German food. It seems as if it is good solid fare, schnitzels and what-not. Anything better than kitekat.

One of the urban myths of my childhood was that Pakistanis in Britain were so poor that they ate cat food. Later I understood this to be nonsense, some mutant form of racial prejudice: cat food was, of course, more expensive than human food. But the equation of poverty and kitekat was now fixed in the imagination of a generation of Englishmen. And now my father was trying to pull on my heartstrings.

Ever since my father had sent me to boarding school, some complicated emotional exchanges had been going on. He thought that I blamed him for sending me to the institution which was in the worst of Victorian traditions. One ritual was to 'bogwash' new boys – shit in the lavatory, then force a new boy's head into the bowl and flush it. The smell, the sense of disgust, never really went. The boys who carried out this torture later became bishops and generals.

Perhaps that is what my father thought he was doing when he sent me to the boarding school: preparing me for the officer class. And perhaps he was right in realising that resentment at a lost childhood had turned me against him.

On holiday from school, he would tell me not to eat so quickly. I would cradle my arms round the bowl of soup or the plate of chicken to show him – in a piece of deceitful melodrama – that school had taught me food could be snatched away at any time. That was not the case but it helped give me an Oliver-Twist image, a sense of victimhood which allowed me subtly to oppress my father.

Now, I could see, he was trying to play the same trick on me. The difference was that we were both adults. The guilt game only worked as a way of articulating resentment from child to parent; it was one of the few weapons available to the weak and the oppressed. So my father was indeed turning himself into a child again, reversing our relationship. The letter was shouting: 'Look after me! Protect me!'

It was too much. I crumpled the letter into a ball, cupping it in my hand as if forming a snowball, before finishing the final sentences.

A drug dealer with spiky unwashed hair and a ring through his lip was now sitting opposite me. On his left arm he had a tattoo in English: Fuck the system. I threw the balled letter at the dealer's recumbent dog (why do all dealers have dogs? Why are they so well-trained?) and prepared to leave the carriage. The dog did not react. But the dealer rose, stooped to pick up my father's missive and carried it to a bin.

'Sorry,' I mumbled, and changed trains.

'Do you think he's mad, I mean clinically insane?' I asked Harry. We were sitting on the steps of the Grunewald house, drinking Beck's two hours later. I had returned just in time to carry the desk and the bed. The rest had been shifted by my colleagues, so I had slipped, guilty as ever, to the supermarket to buy a crate of beer. Tony and the intern were swatting away mosquitoes: Harry seemed immune.

'Nah, it's just an old person thing, I expect. After a while they just can't let go. I mean, look at some of the junk books we've just carried into your place. You should have thrown them away years ago. So you hang on and hang on and the clutter builds up and suddenly you don't have room to breathe so you panic, and the more you panic, the less you can breathe. That's what happens to old people. That's what's happening to your dad. It's normal.'

'Doesn't sound very good to me,' said Tony.

'I don't want to grow old,' said the intern.

'Just keep on saying stupid things like that and your wish will be granted,' growled Tony. Although he was the fittest of all of us, physical effort put him in a foul temper. So did the mosquitoes which were plaguing the city, hovering over the brackish lakes in the turgid heat.

'Bloody global warming,' said Harry. 'It's beginning to get on my nerves.'

Global warming was the explanation for everything this summer. Across Germany rivers were breaking their banks, swollen by monsoon rains. For the mosquitoes, it was a kind of sex paradise. The combination of dirty floodwater, sun and damp had created an Ibiza for mosquitoes.

But for mere humans too there was something epochal, something Biblical about dramatic weather. We all felt we were living in a time of change. Meanwhile, the freshly-painted walls of the flat were beginning to resemble a Rauschenberg exhibition. A spot of blood, certainly mine, in one corner; a separated wing in another. And everywhere bits of the magazine we'd been using to splatter our enemies. Plainly, there was still a role for the printed press in the age of the Internet.

My friends did not really want to hear about my emotionally-sticky dealings with Dad. As far as they were concerned, old people were clapped out machines. They had their own problems.

Tony's wife was poised to leave him. Harry, having put most of his savings into Enron shares, had seen most of his retirement fund evaporate. It would have been better, he mused on the steps, if he had spent the money on beer.

'Look at the arithmetic. At least I would have got back the bottle deposit.'

Both men were, in their way, concerned with ageing. Tony, scared by the prospect of loneliness, was wondering what compromises could be made to buy the loyalty of his wife; Harry, scared by poverty, was always calculating two steps, and two decades ahead. What do I have to invest now, he was constantly brooding, in order to live well at sixty?

But neither made the imaginative leap forward: what kind of person will I be when I am old? How will my personality change? How will my body crumble?

These had not been my concerns either, until my father had nudged his way back into my life. We were the generation of the leasing contract, the monthly payment plan. What happened to your photocopying machine when sixty monthly payments were complete? It was recycled, sent to photocopier heaven and replaced with a newer model. There was no concept, for us, of a life in decay.

The new apartment was the ground floor of a house used as a dancing school by Isadora Duncan and her sister. Their goal, at the beginning of the twentieth century, was to educate impoverished girls from Berlin, and give them a nobility of spirit through dance. She had chosen the place well. With its high stuccoed ceilings and parquet floor, it seemed to develop a human pulse when music was played and the sun dappled the furniture and the unopened cartons.

Tony had set up the sound system and was playing his favourite album, *The Dark Side of the Moon*, at a terrifyingly high volume. We identified the apartment with Isadora Duncan – it was dominated by the former music room and the dancing floor – but the truth was that the house had seen, in 150 years or more, a dozen humans come and go: short lives, long lives, happy people and those immersed in tragedy. Houses sponged up human tears.

For once, it was not only Tony who was clutched by melancholy. We sat silently, interrupted only by the gibbering of the intern and the loud slap of an open palm on mosquito-bitten flesh.

'Bastard!' Buzz. Swat.

'Swine!' Buzz. Swat.

'Hello? Heellloo?' The voice came from the gate. 'Will your truck be parked out there for much longer?'

'My God,' said Harry, 'is global warming making people colour blind?'

He was referring to a strange apparition, a rage of conflicting colour schemes, but instantly recognisable as a version of the new urban German hero: the biking storm-trooper. Helmet in pine green, orange-coloured Pearl Izumi zip-up jacket, skin-tight shiny trousers (similar to those worn by my grandmother when she had a bladder infection) and shaved legs. It was obvious – from smell alone – that he had just been riding his mountain bike forty kilometres in the Grunewald forest. More: that he would soon be on his way to the office where he would wear his uniform until midday, hoping for favourable comment from the secretaries. His bike was parked, with the care usually reserved for Ming-Dynasty vases, on the other side of the road from the removal truck. There did not seem to be a major traffic dilemma. The cyclist jumped easily over the wrought-iron fence and bounded up the steps to the front door. We were too exhausted by this acrobatic display to stand when he offered his gloved hand.

'Braun!' he said. 'Hartmut. I live next door.' He pointed to the big, mid-1990s town house that overlooked my kitchen and my bedroom. In the course of a frayed morning of back-wrenching furniture moving I had swapped a Serbian neighbour who wore a false beard to evade justice, for a rich cyclist with unhealthily tight Lycra trousers and waxed calves.

'Welcome to our street,' he said.

'Thank you,' I said, trying to muster the necessary enthusiasm.

'Are you the mayor, then?' asked Harry.

'Hah, hah! You must be British!'

'No, English,' said Harry.

'And Welsh,' said Tony.

'Hah, hah! I know what you are saying. I too am a Bavarian: A foreigner in Berlin.'

It was clear to me that I should make an effort to be nice. Neighbours were important. The 'Kiez', what American rappers call the 'hood', was the hub of the German universe. The man, though ridiculously dressed, was trying hard. Since I couldn't afford curtains he would soon be able to peer onto my unmade bed from his balcony.

Yet the emotional freight of the day – above all, the anguished and confused letter from my father – had made me snappy.

I was about to ask Herr Braun to leave when I saw the orange rubbish truck edge past our furniture van. The rubbish truck plastered with ridiculous slogans ('We are the dust busters!') was already a familiar sight. It had been methodically cleaning the street, inching noisily forward.

With Wagnerian brio – the shouts of the men in orange, the clanking gears, the whoosh of the rotating brushes – the cleaning truck scraped past our van. And snagged Herr Braun's bicycle, carrying it a metre or two. There was a sickly crunch and I knew that its mountain trekking days were over.

A small, unworthy smile flitted across my face.

Herr Braun, in full verbal flow, had noticed nothing.

'You must meet my wife.'

'Yes,' I said, thinking: if he turns round now he will see the mangled wreckage of his beloved bike. 'I would like that.'

'And here she is.' A tall woman with the slightly bow legs of a cowboy joined us, slapping her husband on the shoulder.

'Sorry, I couldn't join you earlier,' she said in English, 'had to feed the cat.'

Mac's ears cocked, like a gun-dog's. He could recognise a dozen words, but his favourite was CAT.

'This is Hera,' said Hartmut, and it did not seem a coincidence that their names began with the same letter. They were dressed in the same neon colours, they both had wide mouths resembling duck-bills; plainly they both shared the same hobby.

It was, one could see at the outset, a symbiotic relationship. No doubt when Hera suffered period pains, Hartmut had stomach trouble; when Hartmut felt a twinge in the knee, Hera's shoulder twitched.

The Brauns chatted, quietly trying to position me in their universe. Was I married, did I have children, was I rich, was I healthy, how intimate would our relationship be?

None of these questions were openly posed but were part of a subtle reconnaissance.

They worked as a team, smoothly feeding each other conversational ploys. The Brauns were masters not only of two-wheeled locomotion but also of the game of neighbourhood intelligence gathering. They discovered more about me in twenty minutes than a London neighbour would find out in twenty months.

'That's enough!' said Hartmut after a while. 'We mustn't keep you from moving in.'

'Just call if you need a drill hammer or something,' said Hera.

The patter continued for a while until Harry inserted, rather nastily I thought, 'Well, ride home safely then.'

Still blissfully unaware that Hartmut's bike had been mangled, the couple left, cheerfully waving, with promises of dinner.

We left the porch and headed indoors, into the chaos of unpacked cartons. I found a pan and started to fry some eggs for my furniture-removal team. It was time to raise our cholesterol levels.

'Nice couple,' I said.

'Wouldn't trust them,' said Tony, searching among the jumble of boxes for the Black Sabbath CD. 'Too happy. Hiding something under their absurd clothing.'

'Nonsense,' said Harry. 'With Germans like that, what you see is what you get. They just want everything to conform to a kind of suburban order.'

He put on the Harrods souvenir cooking apron and started to croak in imitation of Liza Minnelli: '*Ordnung* makes the world go round, the world go round!'

He flung his left leg out, then his right – a red-faced, middle-aged, hairy-legged version of a chorus girl.

The dog looked frightened.

'You're drunk,' said Tony, echoing my thoughts.

'No, I'm not. All anybody wants is a sense that things should be in their correct place. I mean that's all your dad wants for you too. Life has to have order. That's why the Brauns were asking you those questions – they think a woman brings order and rhythm to the life of a man.'

'Very wise,' I said, thinking: Harry might be a modern-day John Bull, but he really understands the Germans, likes them even. I could see him settling down here, a stranger somehow at home in a strange land. It was left to Tony to do the ethnocentric stereotyping.

'Well,' he said, with grindingly slow deliberation like a Sunday School teacher, 'I think it's an improvement. It's a sign of progress that Germans are no longer seeking to impose order on the world with Prussian grenadiers but are concentrating their testosterone on finding the perfectly compatible woman.'

Harry and I were dumbfounded. It was the longest sentence that we had ever heard Tony speak.

'Oh, shut up, Tony.'

'Yeah, shut up.'

Outside we heard a high-pitched scream of dismay. Hartmut had discovered his bike. We each shook our heads, like sages whose gloomy prophecies had been confirmed.

'Perhaps you should get a mountain bike,' said Harry.

'Don't be ridiculous. There are no mountains in Berlin.'

'You've got to get fit. If you want to get hitched up to a German woman, you've got to get in shape. You don't want to end up looking like Helmut Kohl, do you? Making love to him must be like having a wardrobe falling on top of you.'

'With a key still inside,' added Tony helpfully.

'Take a look at yourself, for God's sake.'

I stood up reluctantly and walked to the full-length mirrors that were in Isadora Duncan's old dancing area. My body did not seem too upsettingly large. A little flabby perhaps. Soft in places. Unappetisingly pale, one could argue. It was all a matter of taste. I twirled round like one of Isadora's ballet students.

No, it didn't look good.

Chapter 7

A Cross Trainer

There are three ways of changing your body shape in Berlin. The first involves radically altering your lifestyle: getting up early, eating cabbage, drinking water out of plastic bottles and adopting a positivist outlook. This was plainly unacceptable.

The second was to go under the knife. Harry and I would sometimes sit in a smart Berlin cafe and play the Botox game, matching fast cars with cosmetic operations: the Jaguar with the facelift, the blue Porsche with the enhanced lips.

It helped us pass the time on a slow weekday morning, and it helped us decode this strange city. Why did so many actresses disappear to spas in April? Answer: out-of-town liposuction so that the scars healed in time for the bikini season.

Of course, you can also be face-lifted and nose-jobbed in Berlin but then you ran the danger of being seen with bloody eyes or a bandaged nose. Better by far to disappear quietly from the capital and return with a dramatic flourish to the fashionable haunts.

So, yes, I suppose I could have my body surgically reshaped to capture the necessary German spouse. But could I afford it? No. Could I stand the pain? No.

Which left the third option: exercise that did not change one's lifestyle but that merely extended it to new areas.

Berlin had two fashionable gyms. One based in the west, was called Asphyxia. Its main rival, Hysteria, was in a luxurious corner of the east. They scrapped with each other like street gangs trying to control their hood.

One would sign up a TV news reader, offering her huge discounts. A week later the rival club would quietly let it be known that a certain diaphanous talk-show hostess had been seen in its steam bath. Since most people were curious to view television personalities naked, and since the changing rooms actively encouraged nudity, the two gyms were the hottest places in town.

Harry went, of course, to sweat off the beer, to punish himself for punishing his liver. It was a deeply Calvinist, psychologically unhealthy motivation. Most gym members are, in fact, emotionally sick; sixty-two per cent according to the Journal of Obesity, a chunky academic periodical. Even so Harry persuaded me that joining a gym was the least painful way of searching for a mate. I became an Asphyxia Man.

It was early on Saturday morning, and the mayor of Berlin was plodding heavily on a running machine. The Israeli ambassador, wiry and grey bearded, was in clear violation of the Sabbath rules by engaging in mortal combat with a machine called a cross trainer. His two bodyguards looked exhausted. I tried to deduce where they carried their guns. The Mayor was obviously curious too and kept staring at their shorts. Next to me on the bikes were two starlets. One was famous for selling ultrasound pictures of her unborn baby to the tabloids. The other, who had big hands like a farmer, was famous for eating maggots on television. They were complaining loudly about men.

Maggot-eater: 'Their hygiene is atrocious.'

Ultrasound: 'They don't even wash their trousers.'

Maggot-eater: 'You're telling me! I had my face in the lap of you-know-who yesterday and...'

Ultrasound: 'At Borchardt's?'

Maggot-eater: 'No, Bocca di Bacco.'

Ultrasound: 'Nobody noticed?'

Maggot-eater: 'Only Luigi.'

Ultrasound: 'He's a darling, my favourite waiter all the time.'

Maggot-eater: 'Anyway, the trousers, they smelled of fish and sweat and earwax and...'

Ultrasound: 'Earwax?'

The starlets turned suddenly, like deer disturbed by the rustling of the forest. A woman, beautiful in her ferocity, was marching towards them. She wore a sleeveless vest and shorts exposing the firm arms and legs of a kick boxer. Her eyes glowed, her nostrils flared in anticipation of a showdown.

'Would you keep your voices down,' she said. It was not a question.

'What's your problem, dear?' asked Maggot-eater, her fitness-centre jewellery jangling. 'Not enough sex?'

The whole room fell silent. Everyone suddenly found the mute MTV and CNN television screens of compelling fascination. The mayor pretended to be gripped by the on-screen hurricane report but slowed his cart-horse tramping to a gentle trot. He did not want to miss a thing, not least because he liked to party with the Maggot-eater and indeed anyone who appeared on reality television.

'No problem that wouldn't be solved by throwing you out of the window, you crone,' said the alert young woman. 'We take our bodies seriously here – it's not the bloody Kit-Kat Club.' The reference was to Berlin's most grotesque sex-club, *the* place to be flogged on a crucifix.

'And what would you know about that, you silly police woman?' spat the Maggot-eater. She dismounted from the bike, smoothed down her skin-tight leopard leggings and turned to Ultrasound. 'Come on, darling. Let's get out of this convent.'

'Try the zoo,' said their beautiful critic.

As the starlets flounced towards the changing room, I folded up my newspaper and walked over to the woman who had so successfully expelled them from carb-burning paradise.

'You're amazing. I've never heard anyone get the last word on the Maggot-eater.'

She turned to me, unsmiling, still red with indignation.

'I can't stand this decadence, this verbal exhibitionism.'

'No, nor can I. But it's quite good fun, isn't it?'

The anger returned to her eyes and then faded.

'You're English, aren't you? That was… irony.'

'Er, yes, I suppose so.'

Harry, as so often before, ambled over to save the moment.

'Well, that was quite a cat fight! Shall we go for a smoke?'

Smoking is punishable by defenestration in Asphyxia where the motto is 'Clean Living – Clean Lungs – Clean the Toilets After You'. On the roof terrace, however, there was a tight corner hidden by potted conifers where you could smoke, cupping your hand to conceal the glow like partisans hiding in the forest.

'Yes, why not?' said the woman to our astonishment. She went up in my estimation – a German woman willing to fight for her principles and still break the rules.

'What's your name?'

'Claudia.'

'Pleased to meet you, Claudia,' said Harry. 'Now let's have a fag. I've had enough excitement for one day.'

So, ostentatously staring into the middle distance, we made our way through the changing rooms where men were striding round naked. The full range of German sausage was on display, from stubby Teewurst to wrinkled cabanos, from frankfurters to Bavarian whitewurst. It was like a cannibal's birthday party. Upstairs, Claudia was waiting for us, sipping a seven euro Kiwi Fitness-Elixir with wholewheat bran. We made our way past more naked flesh – women with dimpled bottoms trying to catch some of Berlin's fading sun – to our smokers' hideaway.

'God, I needed that,' said Claudia exhaling a blue cloud. She obviously also needed to release her anger. 'These women have no self-worth. What's going on with this society? People just sell themselves to television. They want television to do their living for them.' Claudia was breathing fast now. I was afraid she would breathe in some smoke, start to cough and betray our secret den. Her eyes had grown big and round, like fried eggs. There was madness in her. But also a coiled sexuality. Her brown leg was cocked against a plant pot; she smoked hard, like a soldier. She was, I decided, very attractive.

'These women today, what they do to their bodies, then selling their sex-tales to the tabloids, it is just prostitution. I think if we are going to stop the rot then we have to start with our bodies, take control of them, turn them into, I don't know, temples. We should worship our bodies.'

I looked over at Harry, who rolled his eyes. There was no doubt about it: she was crazy. And sexy.

'Isn't that sort of fascist,' I said, 'I mean, like, get a perfect body and you can create a perfect society? I don't much like Maggot-eater and her friend but it sounds a bit like you want to send them to a work camp.'

'No point,' said Harry, 'they'd probably make a TV show out of it.'

'After all,' I said, convinced I was presenting a clinching argument, 'even if you had a perfect body – and yours is pretty good Claudia, if you don't mind me saying so – your ethical apparatus is still likely to be imperfect. Look at Arnie Schwarzenegger.'

'Or Marilyn Monroe,' chipped in Harry. 'Or Raquel Welsh. Or Senta Berger. Or Ursula Andress.'

'Who?' asked Claudia, genuinely baffled by this excursion into the 1970s. 'Look, I'm not saying the problem is that the people are ugly – it's just that they are behaving ugly. They don't respect themselves and that bothers me as a woman.'

'Do you want to ponder this over a bite to eat?' I asked. Claudia paused, looked carefully at me and slowly nodded. Then she stabbed out her Marlboro Light near the roots of the tree as if trying to kill it.

'God, I wouldn't want to get on the wrong side of her,' whispered Harry.

Somehow along the way we lost Harry. His mobile rang – 'Scotland the Brave' – and he drifted off, waving his hand vaguely towards us as we walked towards Benito's. It was a fashionable Italian restaurant with red-and-white check tablecloths, a chrome pasta-making machine in the centre of the room and black-and-white photographs of Marcello Mastroianni. The waiters wore black shirts and pigtails. Over a plate of mussels, it became clear that Claudia was everything that I was not: she was good with computers, she cared passionately about global warming, she believed in a code of modern ethics. The evil of our era, she said, was inconsistency. Yes, George Bush could bomb Iraq in pursuit of an ideal of justice but only if he bombed Iran and Syria and every other dictatorship. And only if he declared his intention in advance.

'In writing,' I said, nodding eagerly. 'In triplicate.'

'Principles are so important,' she said, cracking open a dissident mussel. It sounded like a bone breaking.

'Even destructive ones,' I chipped in.

She glowered at me.

'As for relationships, they should be based on absolute honesty.' Claudia's gaze met mine, as if daring me to flinch. Classic interrogator's tactics.

'Absolutely,' I said, hesitating perhaps a little too long.

'Take you. You are overweight. You don't stand up straight. You have blackheads on your nose.'

I nodded uncertainly, watching her fingers claw in the bowl for another mussel.

'Yet, I find you strangely attractive.'

'Well, that's very forthright of you,' I said, my eyes still focussed on her long fingers. Even they seemed to have muscles as if they had a separate exercise routine. 'Great thing, honesty.'

'I could imagine waking up with you.'

'Gosh.'

'But I need to know that you respect yourself. That you take your body seriously. Because then you will respect me. And take my body seriously.'

'Hmm,' I gulped. I didn't quite follow the drift. Perhaps it was a question of language. I studied the light down on her forearms. 'Well, Claudia,' I said, finally looking her in the eyes. 'You're jolly nice. Very attractive woman and all that. But, you know, we've only just met. Isn't it a bit early to talk about blackheads? And sex. I'm a tiny bit conservative. English, you know. Sorry.'

Claudia was not a listener.

'What you need is a challenge,' she said. 'Like your King Arthur and his knights. Or the ancient Greeks. I shall send you out on a mission to see if you are worthy of me.'

My phone rang. It was Harry.

'Thought it best to leave you two alone.'

I excused myself from Claudia. 'Sorry, it's the bloody office.'

I walked past the blackboard with the chalked-up dishes, past a gossip columnist eating loudly with a schoolgirl admirer and sat next to a pile of dog-eared Italian magazines. *Gente* was speculating about a royal pregnancy.

'Harry, she should be put in a straitjacket.'

'A proper place for a woman, my boy.'

'But she's lock-her-up-and-throw-away-the-key mad. She's probably escaped from some clinic.'

'It was you who invited her for dinner in the first place. And do I have to remind you – you are not the most eligible bachelor in Germany, or indeed on your street?'

'She just told me that. She has a thing about honesty.'

'Pity. But you can't be fussy. The tax year ends in six months. For God's sake, just do what she says.'

Chastened, I returned to Claudia. She switched on a radiant smile displaying a row of sharp, carnivorous teeth.

'I've thought of a challenge for you. You could run the Berlin marathon!'

My stomach felt as if it had just been detached from my body, strapped to an anchor and thrown to the bottom of the ocean.

'That's a great idea,' I lied. 'But I don't think King Arthur would have approved.'

Claudia leaned in close to me.

'*I* will approve.'

Harry and I talked it through the following day over a plate full of pork knuckle. He was, as usual, the Grand Vizier of Deceit, the Prime Minister of Land of Lies.

'Do it,' he said.

'Have you any idea how long the marathon is?'

'Yeah, just googled it. Forty-two kilometres. Named after the Battle of Marathon, 490 BC. The Athenians beat the Persians and some Greek ran for two days to bring news of the victory to Athens.'

'You see, she's got her classical references all mixed up. Why do I have to re-fight a battle in order to earn her love?

She should set a task or something, not put my life at risk. Do you think I should negotiate with her? I mean, I could fly easyJet to Milan and get her the latest Prada boots. Or I could write her a poem. Or buy her the Robbie Williams album. What kind of woman wants me to self-destruct in order to qualify for a relationship?'

'It's perverse,' agreed Harry, mopping up the gravy with a sponge of bread. 'What does she do in real life? Some kind of dominatrix?'

'Politics. She's spokeswoman for a Green Party working group.'

'Thought so.' He snapped his fingers for another beer. The waitress looked annoyed. 'It's obviously about power and control. She wants to make you jump through hoops. So you have to be smart. You have to make her think you are complying, give her the satisfaction of an imaginary victory, while actually keeping control yourself. It's politics, isn't it? Machiavelli. Merkel.'

'Sounds like lying to me.'

'Oh, for God sake, get a grip, mate. You're a journalist. Our whole bloody profession is smoke and mirrors.'

Harry was right again. I tried snapping my fingers for the waitress but it didn't work.

'You have to create the illusion of running a marathon. That's all.' He took out an expensive Mont Blanc pen and started to write on a paper napkin.

The plan was simple: I would register for the marathon. Investment: seventy euros. I would pretend to train. And, sadly, just before the race, Claudia would be called out of Berlin and would be unable to witness the great event.

'What if she reads the list of participants and doesn't find my name?'

'She won't. There are fifty-thousand runners.'

'How are we going to get her out of Berlin?'

'We'll work on it.'

The next day I visited Niketown, perhaps the most irritating shop in Berlin, and bought a pair of silver Road-Runner Specials. They looked like miniature spaceships and cost €212, enough to feed an Ethiopian family for a month. I kept the receipt for the Inland Revenue.

'I've started training,' I told Claudia by telephone.

'Seeing is believing,' she said with a light sprinkling of scepticism. There was, in fact, an air of general disbelief in the Berlin press corps that I should suddenly cast aside my Churchillian convictions (sport is murder) and do something quite as ridiculous as run through the streets. 'Berlin has the cheapest taxis in Europe,' said an unhelpful colleague. 'Why bother?'

The sceptics were not, of course, privy to the Harry masterplan. On the evenings that Claudia did not have to take part in earnest debates about female circumcision or animal cruelty, I would drop by her apartment in running gear. We would exchange a few words about politics, the world. Claudia would be strangely shy at these moments, sizing me up but also thinking perhaps: what have I got into here? I'm sending an unfit man into the near-death experience of a marathon. I clicked my fingers and he came running.

As for me, I felt I was basking in the approval of an attractive woman. A good feeling. So I would bound like a

Labrador with a weak bladder down the four floors of her apartment block and jog at a brisk pace towards the local park, round two corners and into the pub.

'We'll give it two hours,' said Harry, waiting at the corner table with two tall glasses of Pils. Like an authentic trainer, he would lay his stopwatch on the tablecloth alongside a packet of Fisherman's Friends. After a couple of rigorously timed beers, Harry handed me the strong mints. 'Just as well she's not kissing you – these mints would blow her through the wall.' Back up Claudia's steps, two at a time, to work up a sweat. Half a small bottle of Evian poured over my head for that last authentic touch. Then ring the bell.

'God, you look a wreck.'

'Good time,' I would pant, 'two hours, twelve minutes. Getting better.'

'You should be careful, you're overdoing it.'

'No (pant, pant), a challenge is a challenge.'

'Do you want to come in?'

'No, work to do,' I said, 'sorry.' Thinking: yes, actually, I would really like to see how you live. Women have their secret gardens; gain entry and you understand them. Also, I needed to go to the lavatory. Harry's training beers were pressing on my bladder.

'Are you sure?' There was a new softness to her tone.

She wanted to reward me, perhaps, for my extravagant efforts to please her. In truth, I had never strained so hard to attain a woman's approval. Even when I was wooing Becky, I stopped giving flowers after the third week. She said it made her apartment smell like a funeral home. After that any romantic gesture seemed superfluous.

But with Claudia it was different. I really did want to please her, have her stroke my hair and honour my stamina. Perhaps this was more than a tax dodge.

'Well, OK, just quickly. Have to work you know.'

Claudia turned and padded down the corridor. I could see the outline of her back muscles through her thin, sleeveless t-shirt. The walls of the corridor were lined with Russian Futurist posters, more high-brow taste than I had expected; more Spartan too.

Greens, of course, felt an absolute compulsion to advertise their intellectual credentials but I had not marked her down as an environmental radical. She smoked in Asphyxia! She ran a gas-guzzling Chevy – an American car, for God's sake. There was no greater sin, no more obvious perversion of the Green-ethic. She might as well personally chop down the Amazon rainforest or store uranium in her fridge. No, Claudia was a woman of contradictions: I liked her stubbornness.

'Er, Claudia, can I just quickly use your loo?'

She nodded.

'I'll get some wine.'

The lavatory had, in the German manner, a cartoon to demonstrate that this was the home of someone with a sense of humour, the ultimate bourgeois accessory. The cartoon showed a woman cutting a man's tie.

I leaned in to read the small print of the punchline and found myself peeing round the toilet. Grabbing a few sheets of lavatory paper, I wiped it up.

The roll ran out and but there were still some incriminating drops. Could I use her towel? No, no. Her face cloth? No, a thousand times, no. Fortunately there was a copy of *taz*, a left-wing newspaper, lying on the laundry basket. The paper was very absorbent. I washed my hands, noting with approval Claudia's razor: no nonsense about the feminist authenticity of armpit hair.

'Ah,' she said, seeing the crumpled, soggy, pulped up *taz*, 'you've been reading the piece about Nicaragua.'

'Yes, intriguing.'

'Well, sit down in the living room. Shall I throw away that paper?'

'Er, no, I think I'll take it with me. Fascinating article I want to finish.'

'About?'

'About erotic relationships between the English and the Germans.'

'Really? In *taz*?' She looked sceptical.

Taz was the *Izvestia* of the Greens, their organ. Every day it struggled to be funny. It was 'alternative' without understanding the word. And it was very prudish about sex, buttoned up like a nineteenth-century nanny.

'Well, no, not really. I think I was just trying to say that I find you very…' I moved closer so that I could feel her body warmth, smell the animal in the woman.

Suddenly, I remembered why I found her presence so compelling. It was the musky promise – and the feeling that she was in absolute control. Nothing would happen, truly happen, with Claudia until she permitted it.

'I've got you a Chianti.'

'To be honest,' I lied, 'I'm off alcohol. You know, because of the marathon training.'

We were sitting on a dark red sofa. The room was not quite what I had expected; it had none of the austerity of the corridor or the silliness of the bathroom. Moroccan lamps made out of tin or some light metal subtly lit up a room full of warm-coloured drapes: ochre, saffron, reds, yellows and blues. An ornate low-slung table, also from the Maghreb, was surrounded by floor cushions. The effect was of a boudoir, though Claudia may have seen it as a temple to the shrine of multiculturalism. It gave a glimpse of the sensuality that Claudia could not show in public – if she was to be taken seriously in the political establishment.

'I like it here,' I said, which is just about as passionate as an Englishman becomes. I slipped a Fisherman's Friend into my mouth to mask the earlier beer. Drinking beer always made my breath smell like a polluted river.

Claudia was looking at me through the Moroccan haze. The tension crackled between us. I leaned in towards her, knowing that the moment had come. Her mouth – lips narrower than Renata's, but still pneumatically full – edged closer.

'Have you been eating mints again?'

The controlling Claudia had suddenly taken over from the sensual Claudia, like the change of guard in front of Buckingham Palace.

'Helps the concentration.'

Claudia stood up abruptly, brushing imaginary crumbs off her trousers.

'Can you take the rubbish bag down when you go?' A leaking blue plastic bag had been dumped outside the kitchen. I could see the bulging shapes of politically-incorrect plastic bottles and detergents.

'Not very "green", the bag.'

'Not very English, the man,' she replied and shepherded me firmly out the door.

I began to feel easier about the marathon subterfuge. Claudia announced that she wouldn't be there, sadly, but she would be there in spirit and she was very proud of me. She would try to listen to it on the radio and we would meet the next day. She felt sure that our relationship was right and it had been worth waiting for. The words rolled out in a crazy avalanche. She said I had 'integrity'. Sounded fine.

My ego boosted, my tax problems on the road to recovery, I felt OK. For a brief moment I even considered actually running the marathon. The thought quickly passed. A flurry of work distracted me from the looming physical challenge. The business editor decided, probably after drinking too much port, that Germany had a different concept of competition from the rest of the world. 'All this talk of the Anglo-Saxon model and the European social model is nonsense!' he barked over the phone. 'The Germans simply tick differently!' I sighed, but only after putting down the receiver. If I was going to be sent on an absurd mission, I could at least enjoy myself.

So I travelled to Herzogenaurach, a village in Bavaria where Adidas and Puma, the two big running shoe manufacturers, had their factories. They were competing in the world markets yet they did not want to let each other out of sight. In one small town, there were Adidas cafes and Puma cafes: shoe secrets were exchanged on park benches. It was very strange but was it Germanically strange? I came back to Berlin with two free pairs of running shoes. Harry recommended that I donate them to charity. 'Try the Princess Diana Help Fund for Victims of Landmines,' he suggested with a trace of cruelty, 'that way your gift stretches further.' In Berlin I found Greek restaurants next to each other, rival ice cream salons, competing Chinese massage parlours. I tried them all

– the souvlaki, the pistachio ice cream, the foot reflexology – and came to the conclusion: Germans regard competition as sinful, as intrinsically unfair, and so competitors cluster together for warmth. Winning is a cause for shame (what have we done to deserve this?) rather than rejoicing. Germans have a defeatist gene. My boss agreed and liked the article so much that he paid for the massages and banana splits. Not for the Greek food, though.

'The Greeks do not know how to eat,' he snarled. Harry approved of the thesis.

'It's the key to this marathon,' he said, as we slurped our way through a thick pea soup. 'They will do their best to win but secretly feel they deserve to lose. That's why the worst job in Germany is the national football trainer. He can never please his people.'

'So you're saying that the Germans secretly want me to win this bloody marathon? I don't think I'm quite ready for that.' I had, in fact, weighed myself again that morning: another half kilo of body mass, probably fat rather than muscle, had been added over the past week.

Harry shook his head; there were flecks of the thick green soup on his dashing Clark Gable moustache, as if he had blown his nose unsuccessfully.

'It's just that nobody will be expecting you to cheat. They'll just assume that a flabby Englishman is somehow more likely to do well than a fit-as-a-fiddle German.'

'I've never really thought of myself as a cheat.'

'You're not, you're a romantic,' said Harry firmly. 'You're a pragmatist. You're on a quest. It's like they always say: the English are sea-people, the Germans are forest-people. We are risk-takers. We head for the open seas, explorers.'

'Pirates,' I chipped in wanting to put a lid on the simmering hotpot of clichés. 'So, I'm a True Brit, then?'

'That's it. A real Englishman.'

Now, if I correctly understand the Interpol 'wanted' poster for the fugitive Englishman, he is not only a charming rogue who deliberately bends the rules to his advantage, he also reacts quickly in a crisis. He thinks on his feet. The test of this Englishman's mettle came four days before the start of the marathon. Claudia rang. The Greens were in trouble. A respected member of the presidium had been photographed in the new Emporio Armani shop buying a high-collared jacket for her girlfriend. The bill had been forwarded to a public-relations company that also lobbied for an electricity producer. From Claudia's confused account it was not altogether clear whether the Greens disapproved more of Armani than of electricity. Either way, there was a problem. A tabloid had the pictures; a bomb was about to explode. An emergency meeting had been called in Berlin. Claudia was expected to be there.

'On Saturday,' she said breathlessly, her usual self-contained calm swept away by politics. 'I won't be able to make that speech in Dinslaken.'

'Well, don't worry about the school,' I said quickly, 'I'll ring them. You have too much on your hands.'

'That's sweet of you. But there is one good thing. I will be able to cheer you in the marathon. The meeting isn't until the evening.'

'Oh, good,' I said in a flat voice. Oh my God, oh my God. 'That's great, really great.'

Harry rose to the challenge.

Surrounded by chain-smoking skat players, we sat in my local, The Flea and the Horse, and worked out a revised plan for the marathon.

'*Ein Engelchen, dunkel,*' he told Ilona, the waitress. *An Angel, dark.* And for a while it seemed to me that he was summoning up occult powers. In fact, he was ordering a variant of German beer. His sixth. I was on Alka-Seltzer. Life, already hugely complicated, had been further muddled by a call from my father: he was now definitely coming to Cologne with other Bomber-Command veterans for some kind of reunion. He expected me to be in attendance. Worse, Tom — notoriously rude and prejudiced — would be there. I could sense that the event would go horribly wrong. First though, I had to survive the marathon. My stomach was knotted with fear.

Harry spread a map of the marathon course over the table, almost knocking down a plastic flower.

'Start and finish are very close, that's what you have to remember with these stupid races,' he said. My mind was not quite as focussed as usual. Instead, looking at the map I was taking in how many streets were involved. The whole length of the Kurfürstendamm, Berlin's main shopping boulevard — walking at my usual pace that could take up most of Saturday afternoon. Or the endless, boring Hohenzollerndamm with its slightly menacing apartment blocks and dental surgeries. Or Torstrasse in the east, with its endless array of rave clubs and kebab shops. Berlin streets are long and straight, as if built by a Roman emperor for chariot races. It did not seem possible that a human could trudge down them all.

'I can't do this,' I blurted out.

'Concentrate,' said Harry sternly. 'The point of the plan is this: you start the race, disappear and then emerge a couple of hours later at the finish. By my calculations, you won't have to run more than four-hundred metres. You make sure that Claudia is at the finishing line and I will take care of the rest. I will have to put together a team.' He took out his pen and started to write silently on a paper napkin. There were ten points. The stuffed cabbage was getting cold.

'Harry,' I said after a while.

He looked up.

'Thanks.'

Harry waved his hand dismissively. 'What are mates for?'

Chapter Eight

Blood and Kisses

Renata rang.

I had given up on her, and I had problems at first placing her voice. She was, I knew from her speed-dating form, from Nuremberg; naughty Nuremberg with its prostitutes hanging out of windows near the city walls, with its Nazi trials and its sinfully greasy little sausages. Yet there was no trace of a south-German accent. She sounded like a cultured American speaking flawless German but drawing out the vowels, stretching them like a linguistic version of yoga. The effect was one of mystery. From where did she really come? It was easy for a fickle foreigner like me to lose concentration in mid-sentence – snapping back when the final verbs arrived, as if travelling on a delayed train – when listening to a German. But Renata managed to squeeze significance into every word.

'I thought I had upset you,' I said, 'when you started to cry like that. I seem to be upsetting people a lot these days.'

'It was nothing,' she said, 'you just reminded me of somebody.'

'Oh dear.'

'Nobody bad. My brother.'

'He's a journalist?' I could have added: is he shabby, unshaven, incompetent with women, an Englishman lost among the Germans? The similarity must have been striking to release tears.

'No, he's dead.'

'Oh dear.' Brother? Dead? The comparison did not bode well. Either I resembled her brother – safe, sexually neutered. Or I resembled a corpse. This was plainly going to be a relationship made in heaven.

'You don't understand. I find you, er, interesting. Otherwise I wouldn't call you. I don't ring strangers and I never, ever make calls out of politeness.' She paused. 'It's just that I'm not very good at expressing myself.'

'Not at all,' I said. Thinking: get on with it, woman.

'I get all pent up and worried about what people want from me. There's always this question, you know, shall I make an effort to meet somebody's expectations, go all out to charm him, and then maybe raise his hopes too far and end up hurting him? Or shall I wait and see what expectations he has of me, not give anything away – and risk hurting or losing him? It all ends up being so complicated that I withdraw completely, then the man thinks I don't want him or that I'm chronically shy.'

God... It was all a bit too heavy for 10.30 on a Sunday morning.

I looked at the kitchen clock. It would soon be time to put the leg of lamb in the oven. I was cooking lunch for Harry and Tony to thank them for helping to move my furniture. The meal was one of my special concoctions: leg of lamb Japanese-style with plenty of seaweed and wasabi.

'The fact is,' continued Renata, in a torrent of self-analysis, 'I am paralysed by the fear of causing pain. I'm like those Indians, the Jains, who wear special sandals so that they don't kill ants. Then, when something happens, sad thoughts come flooding in. And then I cry.'

I switched on the oven to 220 °C.

'Well, Renata,' I said, looking for a few potatoes that did not have green shoots springing from them, 'I'm glad you're not a complicated woman.'

'You're teasing me.'

'No, shall we meet?' There! Ha! I had said the words.

'That's what I'm ringing about. I've got tickets for *Othello* this evening. Are you interested?'

I was.

Tony and Harry were impressed by the sudden acceleration in my search for a financially-compatible partner. They were less impressed by my cooking.

'It has an interesting aftertaste,' said Tony, 'did you add Chanel No 5?'

'That will be the rice wine,' I said through gritted teeth.

'Do the Japanese actually eat lamb?' asked Harry, hiding a grimace. He clearly thought that I had not seen him slip a large chunk of meat to Mac.

'The Chinese do,' said Tony. 'Brilliant race. Look at what they've invented: chop suey, chopsticks, feng shui.' He pointed at my newly-acquired aquarium that, according to ancient Chinese lore, was supposed to bring luck. 'Jackie Chan,' Tony continued.

'Fireworks,' added Harry, 'fortune cookies, gongs.'

The reference to gongs stirred memories of the speed-dating evening.

'How am I going to handle this?' I asked the think tank. 'With two women, I mean.'

'Two birds in the bush are better than one in the hand,' said Harry cryptically. 'Confucius.'

'My key bit of advice,' said Tony, 'is don't cook for them.' He nodded at Mac who was whimpering and contorting his body as if about to retch.

'Look at it this way,' said Harry. 'What would Satan have done in your position?' He held out his hands. I could see one was sticky from meat, suggesting that he too had been secretly feeding Mac under the table.

'A very useful perspective, I always find,' said Tony. 'The Satanic one.'

'Take them both, see what happens. There isn't even a what-do-you-call-it issue.'

'Ethical?' I ventured.

'That's it, ethical. It's a time issue. You have to get a bride quickly. I don't know why you're dawdling.'

'It's not easy.'

'The alternative is bankruptcy. And leaving your dad in the lurch. What's unethical about that?'

'Where are you taking her?' asked Tony.

'The theatre. She's taking me actually.'

'That's nice,' said Harry, 'you've got Claudia for your body, Renata for your brain. In the end you will have to decide: is Germany better for you physically or mentally?'

'At the moment, I'm both a physical and mental wreck.'

'Well, you should start eating properly,' said Tony. Behind him I saw little pieces of meat sinking to the bottom of the aquarium like shark-bait.

Othello, by the standards of contemporary German theatre, was a triumph. Desdemona masturbated openly with a Coca-Cola bottle; buckets of raw meat were dropped from the rafters onto the players, some of whom were dressed in SS uniform. One actor screamed at a theatre critic and threw carrots at the front row. The actor playing Othello stopped in the middle of the first act to urinate. Since Shakespeare had intended Othello to be black, the director had cleverly dressed him all in white. A backing track played the voice of a woman having an orgasm. It was the perfect setting for a first date.

'Well,' I said in the break, 'at least we haven't had bestiality.'

'I saw a duck being tarred-and-feathered outside,' said Renata, 'so perhaps that will be the climax of the second half.'

We found a table in the lobby.

'I like the Desdemona line,' said Renata, 'about men not being gods.'

'How does it go? Something like — we should not expect the tenderness in marriage that we were given before the wedding.'

'True enough. I was married once, you know.'

'Really?' I was genuinely surprised.

'He was a complete philanderer, girlfriend after girlfriend, but that didn't bother me after a while.'

'Aha...'

'Bernd was a 1968er, a student revolutionary. Well, 1973er I suppose. Anyway he thought jealousy was petit bourgeois. Before me, he had a girl who cheated on him all the time. Once she was screwing somebody in their bedroom and he simply sat outside, waiting. Could you imagine doing that?'

I thought about it for ten seconds. 'No.'

'Then he married me, cheated on me just like his girlfriend had once done to him. And expected I would sit outside the door.'

'That's sick.' And thought: poor woman.

'But the weird thing is that I really did kill my jealousy. Not because it's petit bourgeois or whatever but because – like in the play – it's irrational, based on fear and poor self-esteem. Did Desdemona really cheat on Othello? No, it was in his head. Jealousy is weakness and I don't want to be weak.'

I nodded slowly. And thought: perhaps even control-freak Claudia was more sane.

'But after a while, you had enough – and broke up.'

'No, I told you, I killed my jealousy. My life has no space for an Iago or an Othello. We split up because he couldn't stand my brother.'

'Who's dead.'

She gulped and nodded. I braced myself for more tears.

'He died in an accident. It was a terrible shock. I don't know if I will ever get over it.'

'What was his name?' I reached out a hand and touched the tops of her fingers.

'Bernd, like my husband.'

'That must have been confusing.'

'My brother was a big grizzly bear. My husband was bony and vain and a workaholic who danced like a clockwork robot. There was no way of confusing the two Bernds, believe me.'

'I'm sorry about your brother.' I meant it. There was real sorrow inside her, and it touched me, made me want to reach out for her. Becky, my former wife, was a good, trusting person but she was always cynical about my urge to protect emotionally-bruised women. She called me an ambulance-chaser. I called her a heartless bitch. It's amazing how quickly a relationship can crumble when vocabulary like that is being bandied about.

'Me too,' said Renata, sweeping back her hair, which was shaded red, rust and gold. The packet had probably said something like Autumn Beauty. Or perhaps it was natural. Her neck was long and thin, her skin alabaster pale. This, a ready smile and the glowing hair, made her the centre of attention in the foyer. Men pretended to listen to their wives or queue for red wine and pretzels while darting their eyes at her.

'Renata,' I said, leaning in towards her in a vaguely sensitive way, 'don't bloody well cry again.'

She did not and when the bell rang we went calmly in for the second half. I closed my eyes to block out the absurd stage props and director's little vanities – Desdemona had changed into a tight, black, sex-shop basque – and let the German translation of Shakespeare roll over me.

Women and jealousy: it was a complex subject.

There were sulkers, of course: women who chewed on their thin lips and lost enthusiasm for life. Their complaints were unspoken, obliging the man to deduce the source of the problem, make amends and seek reconciliation.

There were the shouters and the screamers, crying and yelling, slamming doors and breaking plates. There were the avengers who embarked on their own flirtation or affair, who left compromising e-mails on the screen or ostentatiously crumpled love letters in the bin.

All three variants were after the same goal: an admission of wrong doing, and the warmth, the passionate warmth of being right.

But there was also a fourth category, that of Renata: the denier. They were the most mysterious. By denying jealousy they were denying love or even pronouncing it dead.

Othello reacted like a man. He strangled the object of his love. Throughout history there were female castrators, of course. But the nearest these women came to Othello was killing love, dismantling it, rather than admitting to the hurt of betrayal. If Renata fell into that category, then it promised to be a very difficult relationship indeed.

But I was ahead of myself. So far we hadn't even held hands. And Tony's advice had been very specific: make a move as if to kiss her during the break, then she will spend the whole of the second half thinking how it would be.

A wise man, Tony.

But I had already lost the moment for the proto-kiss. We had talked too much. Trying to salvage the situation, I waited until Desdemona was speaking to her duplicitous servant. Slowly I stretched out my left hand and took Renata's right. She gripped my hand and slowly, steadily, like a crane transporting rocks in a quarry, lifted it and dropped it back into my lap.

So, I thought, while wiping the sweat of my palm on my trousers – that was a clear message. I concentrated on waiting for Othello to kill his wife. No doubt, in the hands of this befuddled director, it would be a bloody, exhausting affair. There was no room for fantasy in the modern German theatre. I opened my eyes, confirmed my assessment – a bucket of fake blood was about to spill onto a virginal white bed – and glanced surreptitiously at Renata. She was looking at me. With a shy smile, she held my hand and started to stroke each individual finger. In that moment, I forgot Claudia, the dreaded marathon, the tax man and even my telephone which was silently but insistently vibrating in my pocket.

The final curtain came as a relief to most of the audience who dutifully clapped. Renata did not release her hand but signified half-hearted approval by banging the armrest with her left fist. I used my spare hand to check my phone: a text message from Harry requesting a progress report and a missed call from my father.

Even this intrusion was not enough to dampen my ardour, as Rosamund Pilcher would have said. We snow-ploughed our way through the crowd. I spotted Herr Bunger, my local bio-butcher and waved; no doubt he had come for the blood. Renata looked flushed. It was the usual post-performance maelstrom; a scrum round the cloakroom, loud discussion as to where to eat or where the car was parked and long queues for the toilets. For all the obvious biological reasons, the queue for the ladies' was longest and the women sought out the usual displacement activities, moving from foot to foot or burrowing in their handbags for loose change.

'Quick, in here,' said Renata.

'But... ' There was no time to resist. Renata pulled me into the toilet for the handicapped. She cut a slight figure but had broad shoulders that she used with the expertise of a judo-fighter. Her determined nudge pushed me through the door. Renata locked it behind us.

'It's *verboten*, Renata,' I said, 'what if someone wants to use the place? You can't be that desperate.'

It seemed somehow too early in a relationship to watch one's girlfriend – was she even that? – urinating. And was my presence really required?

'Don't be so bloody German,' she said, and grabbed my face with two hands. She had to stand on tiptoes but we managed a serious kiss. I could smell her perfume, her hair; she no doubt smelled my sweat. It was a good kiss; playful tongues, but above all that special warmth of mutual surrender. There was nothing ambiguous or tentative about it. It was a prelude to sex. That kind of kiss. The position was a strain, the difference in height too large for comfort. With a grunt I picked Renata up and sat her on the sink so that we were more or less eye to eye, mouth to mouth. She spread her legs and then hooked round the back of my knees. I clutched her bottom – little patches of water from the sink had soaked into her silk dress – and then held her head as if the join between our mouths would stop us losing balance. I felt a surge of desire. It was the logical sum of the emotions that had accumulated during *Othello*: her physicality, the sound of her breathing next to me in the darkened theatre, the touch, but also the sense of her sorrow, her past hurt, her confusion. It was indeed a very good kiss.

The door rattled. There was an insistent knocking.

'Oh shit,' I gasped. 'Schaeuble.' I had seen the wheelchair-bound German politician in the audience. Plainly he needed to use the special toilet.

We adjusted our clothing.

'What are we going to do?' hissed Renata.

'You keep out of sight. I'll open the door, step back, let the wheelchair in and then while it's manoeuvring, you slip out.' Renata started to comb her hair.

'No time for that,' I said. 'Stand back, I'm going to open the door.'

I flushed the lavatory to give an air of authenticity to the proceedings and flung open the door. Expecting a wheelchair, my gaze was directed downwards. Instead of wheels though I saw a dainty pair of black-patent leather shoes. Slowly I looked up, taking in expensive evening clothes, even a fur stole.

'My God,' said a woman's voice, 'what are you doing here?'

'Frau Beckenbender!' For it was she.

We stood gaping at each other. What would Harry have done? I had to think for myself.

'Terribly sorry, Frau Beckenbender,' I stammered, 'I had to dictate an article over the phone.' I drew the mobile out of my pocket. It was vibrating again, right on cue.

'That will be the newspaper again. A journalist's work is never done.'

'I thought I heard voices.'

'Yes, the reception is always exceptionally good in toilets, especially handicapped toilets.'

'Well, could I perhaps come in. The queue for the ladies' is intolerably long.' I felt Renata tugging on the back of my jacket. She seemed to want me to stall.

'Of course,' I said, taking a half step backwards. 'Did you know my father is coming over?'

'Well, that's splendid, we must meet up again.'

You have to admire the backbone of the older generation. Frau Beckenbender, her physical need obviously urgent, appeared genuinely interested in the imminent arrival of my father.

'I must cook you all dinner,' I said. What was Renata up to?

Frau Beckenbender's face gave an almost imperceptible twitch. 'I think it might be better if I cooked this time. A potato dish perhaps? Now, if you would excuse me... '

I edged past her, hoping that the sheer bulk of my body would hide Renata if she cowered behind me.

Frau Beckenbender however glimpsed a strand of Renata's red hair. She raised an eyebrow.

'Hello,' said Renata, 'I'm the news assistant.'

She held up the toilet brush which she had wrapped with something resembling silver foil that had been stored in her handbag.

'I hold the emergency antenna when he's using the phone. To call London.'

'In handicapped toilets?'

'Yes, quite, in toilets.'

'Well, pleased to meet you. Now if you will excuse me.'

We scrambled out.

Frau Beckenbender began, 'By the way, Miss... '

'Renata.'

'Your dress is undone, Miss Renata.'

Outside, our breathing returned to normal.

'I think that went well, don't you?' I said.

'I didn't know you could cook,' said Renata.

'I didn't know you could kiss. As for my cooking, it's legendary.'

'Legendary, as in not true, you mean?'

'Legendary as in the Rhine Maiden, Lorelei – so seductive it lures people to their deaths.'

Renata threw back her head and laughed.

It occured to me: I had never heard Claudia laugh.

Chapter Nine

Run For Your Wife

I felt queasy. The panic juices in my bowels seemed to be making as much noise as the brass band. They were large men with red noses, sweating over their tubas, but I still would have exchanged my life for theirs. And, if there had been money in my account, I would have thrown in a fat cheque.

'You nervous?' asked Harry. He had a whistle on a chain strung round his neck, a clip board and a spare tracksuit top tied round his swelling front like a butcher's apron. He looked ridiculous. I would have swapped my life with him too.

'No,' I said. 'It's just a bit chilly out.'

'I can see goose pimples on your legs.'

'Well, I'm not used to wearing shorts. Haven't worn them since school.'

'Don't tell anyone that, you're supposed to have been in training for the past three months.' Harry sucked on his biro. 'Can't train without shorts.'

Harry and I sized up the competition. The usual pint-sized African runners milled round modestly bobbing up and down, so obviously the winners I wondered why anyone else bothered. Then there were the other serious runners with headbands and knee guards and little bottles of Evian strapped near their crotches. I recognised one from the cocktail-party circuit, a self-torturing Catholic banker called Ruediger. He had his legs wide apart and was stretching to reach one of them.

'So, the English have come to teach us how to run!' Artificially-whitened teeth flashed an unreliable smile.

'Tortoise and hare,' I called out, 'tortoise and hare.' Ruediger's brow crinkled; he was not a man for fables.

'You might have a bit of trouble with that one,' said Harry. We both laughed out loud. Our marathon was going to be a little less physically demanding than Ruediger's. Intellectually more challenging, though.

The runners started to crowd round the start position as if waiting for the opening of the winter sales. Many looked like escaped convicts, shaven-headed Bruce Willis look-alikes. Perhaps they had spent the last year doing one-armed press-ups in their cells. They smelled of the prison exercise yard – that embrocation cream applied by body-builders – and crisply nodded at each other. No, this was not my natural habitat.

'The quicker we get this bloody thing over with, the better,' I muttered to Harry.

'Think Claudia,' he said. 'Think tax debt.'

It was however difficult to concentrate on Claudia while the memory of Renata's kiss was still fresh. My body was confused by German womanhood.

Was I more attracted to their rationed sensuality, their Claudia-like ability to compartmentalise life? Or to their edgy intellectualism, their bottomless Renata-like capacity to make themselves feel guilty? It was no longer, I realised, about pleasing the Inland Revenue; it was about deciding what I really wanted out of life.

Claudia may have worked out in the gym but it was largely an act of vanity. She commuted, like many of her Green colleagues, between self-indulgence and self-hatred. Claudia liked her car, her body, her cigarettes, good food. Sometimes she decided it was wrong to like these things but rather than give them up, she turned her anger outwards and sought to exercise control over others.

Did I want that? Was it worth running the marathon for? Even a very abbreviated version? Should you cheat to win the approval of someone you're attracted to, but don't particularly like? What kind of masochistic force bound me to her? Was it perhaps the same masochism that kept me living in Germany? A country where – in order to survive financially – I had to cheat the system?

There had been a slight drizzle and the Kenyan super-star was wrapped in a blanket like a little old lady, strangely shrivelled. The preparation for the start seemed to take an age as we were divided into pens. Ruediger was in my group. 'So, are you the tortoise or the hare?' Somehow he had googled Aesop's fables in the past fifteen minutes. I was impressed. He was obviously running with an Internet-linked mobile phone.

'I rather thought we were running against ourselves,' I said, summoning up the pompous tones of a television evangelist. This usually brought people to their knees.

'Yes, yes, of course,' said Ruediger. 'Human endurance, spirit over matter.'

'*Triumph of the Will*,' added Harry. 'Now, if you will excuse us, we've got strategy to discuss.' Ruediger looked confused again. 'Maybe we can run together?' he called out. We ignored him.

'The snapper is in place,' he said. 'Now give me the chip.' I removed the microchip from my shoe and gave it to Harry who moved off into the crowd of runners in search of our secret teammate.

The plan went as follows: I was to run the first 150 metres as fast as I could, as if it were a sprint. With some luck I could be close to the lead runners for a minute or two. Our photographer would take a picture of me, preferably nudging alongside one of the African stars. Then, I would fall back rapidly and slip into the Tiergarten, Berlin's sprawling, leafy central park, feigning a need to vomit. The way I felt at the moment I would not need great acting skills. The idea was to melt into the trees, like Robin Hood. Harry would be waiting with a commandeered rickshaw. The finishing line was about a kilometre through the Tiergarten. We had found – and sabotaged – a portaloo about 300 metres from the Brandenburg Gate. That is where I would hide for two hours. My microchip meanwhile had been attached to the shoe of my intern, Jonathan. There were eleven control points round the marathon course and the chip – my chip – had to cross every one of them. When Jonathan approached the finish, he would give a signal, Harry would give a coded knock on the door of the portaloo and I would enter the final stretch alongside my chip-carrier. 'It's no more immoral,' said Harry, 'than an infertile mother paying someone to have her baby. Ethically debatable, yes, but immoral, no.'

The plan was not infallible but it was touched with a kind of genius. The feeling that a team was in place gave me a (probably false) sense of security. We could have been a platoon in the trenches at Ypres, waiting to go into battle, each aware of our role. I turned round to tell Harry this martial analogy but he had disappeared. He had moved on, up beyond the photographer, towards the pick-up point. I was alone. Confidence melted. I was gripped by an urgent need to go to the lavatory. They probably felt that at Ypres too.

The starter had a straight back and looked as if he knew how to use the starter's pistol in close combat. He reminded me of my father as a younger man, a stickler for the rules. Dad would not have been proud of me today: for his generation it was better to suffer and sweat than take an easy or devious road. That, of course, is why so many of them ended up as young corpses.

'Ready… '

There was a collective intake of breath. I was not the only nervous man in Berlin that day.

'Steady… '

I tried to concentrate on the strategy. I would almost certainly have to elbow aside the runners next to me.

'Go!' The pistol cracked.

We charged forward like dragoons on horses.

'*Vorsicht! Vorsicht!*' shouted two or three runners. 'Careful! Careful!' Somebody had slipped and rolled in front of the crowd, clutching his head to prevent it being flattened by

Nike Super-Lightning running shoes. We hurdled over him and I half wished I had done something similar. Why couldn't I have told Claudia that I had been injured in the race? Surely, she would have accepted the explanation. And probably classified me as a weakling and a loser. All round me men were saying to themselves: shit, shit, shit. Big, grown-up men grunting and cursing. The pace was slow. Most had probably worked out their game plan: slow and steady for the first ten kilometres, then acceleration for another ten. That kind of thing. God knows. I had no calculations beyond 150 metres and I was already panting like a narrow-gauge steam engine after forty metres. With an immense effort of will, I pushed past the pack and started to sprint as if I were about to catch the bus to work. Ahead of me there were small knots of runners, blissfully obstructive.

'Budge!' I hissed at them, 'Emergency Doctor.' As good German citizens, they obeyed reflexively though there was not the slightest logic in a doctor following on their heels. Ruediger was one of the runners and flashed me a look of astonishment as I pushed on past. Faster! Faster! I could see the backs of the frontrunners and their pacemakers. They had settled comfortably into a pace that would carry them on for over forty kilometres. I could perhaps sustain it for another forty seconds. Then I glimpsed the photographer, handsome in a cadaverous way, camera at the ready. I waved to him. I wasn't exactly abreast of the leaders but with some artful camera work he could put me in the same frame. It is remarkable what can be done nowadays with digital photography. He clicked and clicked and then raised his thumb as if to say: you can stop your ridiculous adventure. Not before time. I slowed down and let myself be overtaken by almost a thousand runners including Ruediger who didn't notice me in the crowd. He was pumping forwards, his arms making piston movements. It was like being in a giant nineteenth-century factory surrounded by steam-driven machines. Slowly, barely above walking pace, I peeled off towards the pavement. There was a small group of spectators who gazed me at with sympathy. My face felt hot and swollen to the touch. I probably looked like a pumpkin.

'Shall we call a doctor?' asked one worried woman clutching a mouse-like dog to her ample chest, obviously worried that I was about to explode, splattering her new Barbour jacket with bits of overheated flesh and bone marrow. She was probably right.

'No, it's OK, it's OK,' I panted without any need to embellish my performance. 'I just need to be sick.'

The spectators swiftly cleared a passage and switched their attention to the race. I waded into the bushes, made some loud retching noises, then walked deeper into the Tiergarten, past a gardener's shed, past a gay couple fiddling with each other's leather trousers, into the bucolic heart of Berlin. At last, I saw the signal: an old World Cup T-shirt hoisted on a branch.

'Come on!' hissed Harry from behind a bush. 'Get this on. We've got to get out of here.' He handed me the tracksuit top he had been wearing round his waist. It was important to hide my number and my identity as a marathon runner. Out of a duffel bag he tugged a baseball cap and a pair of jogging pants. The side zips allowed me to pull them over the Nike shoes. Harry looked both ways to make sure the coast was clear and then, with preternatural calm, strolled over to a rickshaw. The Bombay-style taxi had caught on in Berlin, especially with tourists who were too lazy or too stupid to master the S-Bahn network. Most used the rickshaw only once: Berlin roads were in such bad condition that a ride was an exercise in masochism. The passenger was thrown round like a sack of rice. But Harry was right. On marathon day it was the most efficient and most discreet mode of transport. Harry started to pedal. As I studied his bulging buttocks I couldn't help wondering whether he should not put in a bit more exercise. Running, for example.

'Everything's on schedule,' said Harry, gasping a little. 'The intern's on his way round with your microchip. The loo is ready. As soon as he's within sight, I'll knock, you join him and finish together.'

'Great, Harry. You haven't hidden any food in the loo, have you?' The brief physical effort had awakened my appetite.

'A baguette, a brie and a bottle of red wine from the supermarket. I'll send you regular SMS messages so you know how the race is going.'

I patted my pockets and realised I had left my mobile at home.

'Forgotten my phone.'

Silence from Harry. He hated ineffiency.

'That was pretty stupid. Still, we can manage without.'

We had reached the drop-off point without attracting attention. Harry carefully padlocked the rickshaw (Berlin was full of dishonest people). Using our half-remembered boy-scout skills – Harry had been expelled for selling cigarettes – we half crawled, half stumbled to the portaloo. It smelt horribly.

'That's the brie,' said Harry. 'We need to deter other people from using this toilet.' He cast an experienced glance over the Strasse des 17. Juni. 'Not many people yet, too early. And no one will pay any attention to you. Get in quickly.' As I entered the toilet, gagging from the smell of urine, I heard him hang the 'out of order' sign on the outside handle. There were some tired copies of a tabloid next to the cistern, probably in case the lavatory paper ran out. I made myself comfortable.

'Don't open, whoever shouts or rattles the handle. And don't make a squeak. And keep an eye on your watch. I'll be back in about two hours.' Harry sounded a little on edge. I, by contrast, was getting calmer. What could go wrong? 'This will be my knock. Da-da-da-dum.' It was the rhythm from Beethoven's Fifth that had been used by the BBC when it broadcast into Nazi Germany. I realised why Harry was so excited: he saw himself as a member of the resistance in occupied France. Hence the brie.

The air was stale and musty in my hideaway. The papers were read in a matter of minutes. Sitting on the lavatory seat made my stomach rumble; an interesting psychological reflex. I tried to play a game of chess in my head and failed. I ate some brie. I fell asleep.

Da-da-da-dum! The knocking was urgent. The whole metal shed vibrated. It was like being imprisoned in a big bass drum. The watch showed that barely an hour had passed.

'OK, OK, what's the rush?'

Harry was a bag of nerves.

'Your Claudia just rang me,' he wheezed, as if he had been running or cycling.

'Why you?'

'Because you left your mobile at her place, you fool. She wanted to pass on the message: she has decided not to wait at the Brandenburg Gate, but halfway round the course. Says it's closer to the place where she has her meeting. Tried to talk her out of it, but she's very determined.'

'Shit.' It was very uncomfortable with both of us in the loo. 'What are we going to do?'

'Plan B. I drive you as close as we can get, infiltrate a group of runners that passes her, then get you out again, back here in time to join up with the student and then finish as planned.'

'That's a lot more running than you promised.'

'About a kilometre. It'll do you good. I'm the only one who's moved his butt today.'

'Will it work? Sounds a bit risky.'

'Of course it will. Remember, nobody seriously anticipates runners cheating at the marathon. What would be the point?'

'Quite.'

The infiltration point, I discovered, was the noisiest stretch of the marathon. There was a band on a podium playing oompah-oompah music. Spectators had brought horns and whistles. Frightened dogs howled for their masters. Children screamed because the ketchup from their hotdogs had squirted onto their coats. It was as good a place as any to infiltrate unnoticed. By the time that Harry's Mercedes had negotiated its way through the blocked-off streets, the race was being run by the weaker competitors. 'The women, the cripples and the Danes,' said Harry, displaying his special brand of heartlessness. 'You should do just fine.' I had studied the map in Harry's car. Our best bet was for me to plod steadily for a few hundred yards, gallop past Claudia and duck into a pastry shop to use their lavatory. Harry would collect me at the back entrance and take me to the final stretch of the race.

Harry took my tracksuit. I was again a man with a number. 'Now, go for it!' he shouted in my ear and pushed me out of the car towards the road. It was strange to be running again. For a moment, I felt a twinge of regret that I had not just completed twenty or so kilometres like the other racers. A remarkable sense of solidarity seemed to have sprung up. They were no longer racing against each other, but against their own bodies. They smiled at me: a fellow inmate in the asylum. It was not far to Claudia's position but I would still rather have taken a taxi.

From the distance I could make out a red pashmina shawl and knew instinctively that this was Claudia. She had obviously bought a rattle from the bearded peddler selling whistles and hooters to the crowd. It was a strange corner of Berlin, an oasis of ostentatious wealth: a fashionably expensive hairdresser, a kitchen-utensils boutique for women who paid others to cook and the pastry shop where the locals would park their Porsche Cayenne jeeps before dashing in to buy a bag of croissants for breakfast at ten o'clock in the morning. The fans were dressed accordingly; in unseasonable Gucci sunglasses, in green hunting jackets or blue double-breasted blazers over designer jeans. Claudia, plainly, did not fit into this crowd and perhaps for that reason shouted louder than anybody.

'Come on, *der Englaender*,' she yelled, 'You can do it!' She spun her rattle, screamed something resembling an Apache battle cry, and looked absolutely stunning. She would have been worth running twenty-something kilometres for. I gave her a brave wave.

As planned, I peeled away from the runners after I had passed Claudia and stampeded down the steps of the Konditorei as if desperate to use the lavatory. The botoxed actresses looked up from their cheese cakes and nodded approvingly.

'Did you see Claudia?' I whispered to Harry as I climbed yet again into a tracksuit.

'Of course, I bloody did. She just rang me and said she was so worried about the way you looked she was going to head for the finishing line after all.'

'Oh God, we'd better beat her to it.'

'That's fixed. I've scattered a few nails in front of her Chevy. It's public transport for her.'

In the nick of time we slipped onto the final stretch just as Jonathan came into view. 'You took your time,' I said.

'And you've had an easy couple of hours in the pub,' he grimaced.

I barely took in the clapping as I trudged in through the finishing line. My first instinct was to smoke a cigarette and have a beer but this would have rather tarnished the image of the great athlete impatient to claim his laurel wreath. Ruediger had arrived ahead of me, apparently without cheating. He was lying on the pavement, making a pantomime out of his physical suffering. 'Good run!' I told the prone, broken figure, generous in my defeat. I poured a bottle of Evian over his face and he started to stir. 'Didn't think you would finish,' he said, 'You look such shit.' I took this as a compliment.

Then I caught a glimpse of red. It was Claudia marching towards me as I had once seen her advance on an actress who swallowed maggots and talked dirty.

'Hi, Claudia,' I said, thinking: this is the beginning of a new level of physical intimacy. A sweating, unfit man prepares to embrace a perfumed, fit woman.

'You bastard,' she said.

I felt my stomach plunge. How had she found me out? Where had I slipped up? Had I been spotted?

'What do you mean, Claudia? I thought you'd be pleased to see me.' Perhaps Harry had been indiscreet? Or the intern?

'Who,' she said, the anger almost changing the colour of her eyes, 'who is Renata?' She held up my mobile phone to show that she had been reading my text messages.

Chapter Ten

Wet Heroes

'How do I look?'

Old, of course. I had studied Dad earlier, seen the bush of grey hair growing out of his supposedly shaven chin, the patches of stubble on his throat, which had been missed by the razor. There was a light sprinkling of dandruff on the shoulder of his dark military blazer, like icing sugar on poppy cake.

'Fine, just fine.'

I didn't turn round and continued staring at the Cathedral out of the window of the Hotel Excelsior. The sky, typical for a late Rhineland summer, resembled damp brown gabardine. The smell, coming through the crack of the unwashed five-star, €240-a-night window, was wet dog. It had been raining for exactly eleven days. Cologne was at its most beautiful; a widow in grey.

I was still a bit shocked by Dad's physical presence. Despite all the hints, despite the phone calls and the letter, I had not really expected him to come. He had seemed so depressed, so incapable of action.

I could not imagine him setting out on the long trek to Stansted airport, standing in the noisy queue for Proletarian Airlines and making his way past German passport control without provoking some kind of international incident. But I had underestimated him.

When I met him in Cologne, he was predictably frail. Somehow, though, he had charmed the flight attendants – I am old enough to remember when they were called stewardesses – and at least a dozen passengers seemed to be on first name terms with him.

The malign influence of Tom was already obvious. Tom had persuaded the airline to supply them both with wheelchairs to speed their way to the luggage pick-up. Tom admittedly had one leg missing but that hadn't stopped him walking a kilometre to the pub every day or indeed having a number of affairs. As for my father, he had always been a walker, taking time off from my mother and domestic routine to walk across the Yorkshire Dales. Now, I could see, his leg muscles were beginning to wither.

Dad was still staring at the body-length mirror. The army feminises men: no one looks at his reflection as many times a day as a soldier. They adjust the creases of their trousers, cock the angle of their hat. They are as hungry for admiration as a catwalk mannequin. Difficult to imagine them going off later to kill someone. And especially difficult to picture your father killing others.

'Last time we had contact with Cologne, it was at 18,000 feet,' said my father. 'The city was just zone one, zone two, zone three in those days. This would have been zone one, because of the railway station. Isn't that right Tom?'

Tom had been the rear gunner in the Lancaster piloted by my father. He was, if anything, even more vain than Dad. Sitting on the edge of the hotel bed he was twirling the ends of his waxed ginger moustache. I know that he pretended to the barmaid of his local pub in Deal that he had been an officer, a daring pilot. The moustache was part of the pretence: it was an officer's growth, made to point upwards like the handlebars of a mountain bike. Only gay men wax their moustaches nowadays, I had once told him, and he had glared at me as if I had been in the sight of his Browning machine gun.

Tom rose, with difficulty, his arms spread out like wings and made engine noises – vroom, vroom – through his false teeth. He was, as ever, profoundly embarrassing.

'Maybe you shouldn't overdo the bomber imitation this afternoon,' I said. 'You are supposed to be on a reconciliation mission, remember? And you bombed this place flat. I don't think people will laugh too hysterically.'

'You leave Tom alone,' said my father sharply, as if I were a cheeky eleven-year-old. 'We did what we had to do, and they did what they had to do.'

'Aye, only they had camps and stuff,' chipped in Tom.

'Well, you did all right out of your camp, as I recall.'

Both men had been captured when they were shot down over Aachen and had spent the next sixty years telling stories about their adventures, the good guards, the bad guards. As I grew older and started to watch *Hogan's Heroes* I realised that some of the stories had been borrowed from television.

Tom's leg, supposedly lost when his plane was shot down, was actually amputated in 1957 after an unlucky, and very alcoholised, exit from a moving taxi. Those were the days before child safety locks. Even so, their war, compared to the Germans they had bombed, had not been so bad. The prison camp was more comfortable than their boarding school, their food was better than Royal Air Force rations, they caught up with their sleep and they were spared from their demanding girlfriends at home – whom they later went on to marry and impregnate. War, for them, was a second boyhood.

I walked over to my father and brushed some of the snow from his shoulders.

He twitched with irritation: 'Why don't you wait downstairs.'

I was happy to be alone for a while. The need to find a suitable bride was taking its emotional toll. Rarely had I felt so tired. In theory at least I should have been bursting with energy. Following a long, dry period after Becky, I was grappling with a choice between two attractive women.

Claudia's jealousy about Renata had taken me by surprise. It seemed such a strange relationship with Claudia, on and off, full of promise and of promise denied; platonic and yet full of physical potential.

Tony told me, drawing on the long annals of his experience, that this was a normal German relationship.

'German women spend eighty per cent of their time in concealment,' he confided over a well-earned, post-marathon beer. 'They are the Viet Cong of our days. They march by night, hide by day, staging occasional ambushes.'

I thought about this extravagant metaphor for a while.

'So, the answer is to napalm them?' I concluded.

Tony nodded vigorously. 'Or marry them.'

Claudia had calmed down a little. I had, in my masculine way, played down the episode with Renata. And, after all, I had just run a marathon to please her. It was a physical investment in a physical relationship. Not a very honest one, perhaps, but it was at least based on mutual attraction and good will.

We decided to take a short sabbatical from the relationship, let it rest – marinate would be a better word since I had been drinking more systematically since the end of my marathon training – until after I had steered my father through his wartime reunion. Then we would talk sensibly and seriously.

Yet the kiss with Renata had created a bond, greater than that of the near-kiss with Claudia. Renata, full of self-doubt but intellectually alert: I couldn't get her out of my mind. Not least because she was constantly sending me text messages. They had a lightly teasing tone, not exactly flirtatious but demanding attention. She was hungry, it seemed, for conversation even if it was in the crude form of an SMS.

Where it was all going to lead I couldn't tell but there was a clear difference in style between them.

Claudia was a woman who favoured the staccato: off-on, on-off. It was like deciphering a message in Morse code.

Renata flowed; the kiss, I understood, was part of a rolling process. She was an intellectual, in a German arts-page-reading way, but one capable, even eager, to switch off her brain.

What to do?

Choosing one or the other would be a statement about me. Or about my financial status. Time was running out. And how long could my father operate as an independent being? I would have to watch him carefully.

The lobby was beginning to fill up with veterans, already rehearsing their stories. In their own country, they were technically heroes but, in fact, regarded as something of a bore. Or even an embarrassment. Here, they could reconstruct their youth without someone shouting: shut up you old windbag!

'You must be Bob's son,' said a man with Parachute Regiment wings pinned to his lapels.

'That's me,' I strained to look over his shoulder. His breath smelled of sour milk.

'He was blond just like you, curly hair. We called him Angel Face.'

'How did you know him? I mean you were jumping out of planes, weren't you? And he was dropping bombs.'

'Met on leave, summer 1942. Shared the same girlfriend for a while.'

The old paratrooper started to cough until he was red in the face. His nose and cheeks were full of broken veins. One eye seemed to point leftwards.

'Not my mother, I hope.'

'Course not. Great little woman.'

'She died a while back.'

'Sorry to hear it. Elspeth, her name wasn't it?'

'Eileen.'

'Ah, yes.' The paratrooper turned abruptly to go, pushed through the blazers and baggy flannel trousers, towards the toilets.

Dad and Tom arrived. I ignored Tom.

'Who is that parachute chap, Dad? He seems to know you well.'

Dad stared at the man waddling past the reception. 'Never seen him before in my life.'

'He didn't have an affair with Mum, did he?'

'I've told you a hundred times, Mum did not like sex. Now stop talking dirty and count everybody.'

The veterans were all present and, more or less, alive. No heart attacks yet, no one stuck in the lavatory. Buzzing like debutantes at a ball they crowded into the bus, the old pilots sitting towards the front, the gunners at the back, the navigators took window seats.

'*Willkommen in Köln,*' said the young student guide from the Christian charity that was paying the bills. 'Welcome to Cologne.'

'*Willkommen, bienvenue – vel-kom.*' That was Tom and I could sense trouble ahead.

'We are now on our way to the air academy in Hangelar, a little way outside town. There you will meet veterans of the night-fighter squadrons. As you can see from your programmes,' I saw – point 5. 14.30–15.30: spontaneous conversation – 'this will be a highpoint. Let's hope the weather improves! In the meantime, relax and enjoy your tour of reunification!'

Sociologists say that young British and German people have uniquely short attention spans. Only the Americans are worse. But even the non-video game and SMS generations – working mothers in Essen and Leeds, middle managers, city traders, policemen – have astonishingly weak concentration. Worst of all are the over-seventies. They whine, they demand attention and pretend to read books but secretly read *Bild* and the *Daily Mirror*. And that's just the sane ones.

Sure enough, Britain's assorted heroes who were visiting Germany for the first time in sixty years chose not to look out their windows at the new country but rather to launch into a sing-along. 'Hitler has only got one ball – and Goebbels has no balls at all!' they sang, linking arms on the backseat. I spotted Tom at the centre of this subversive activity.

'Dad, please tell Tom sometime that Hitler is dead. Goebbels too.'

'Tried to explain it to him, lad, but all he said was: do we have proof?'

I sighed. On the autobahn there was a big sign marked: Wahn 10 kilometres. Wahn was a suburb of Cologne. It was also, appropriately, the German word for madness.

The smell of roasting beef wafted out from the barracks and engulfed the old Englishmen as they tentatively stepped onto German military terrain. This was, I could see, to be one of those intricately planned friendship missions. A few years ago Germans would rather have chewed carpets than touch beef, tainted by British madness. Now beef was on the menu again and one guessed that the welcoming speeches would make some semi-humorous reference to cows. I could hardly wait.

Outside the academy stood ten men. Ten Germans to fourteen of ours. The odds were good but not conclusive.

'They look bloody fit,' said the parachute veteran who may, or may not, have had a fling with my Mum.

'It's all those holidays in Majorca,' said Tom, and indeed many of the German pilots had brown parchment skin stretched tightly over their cheekbones. All ten stood with their shoulders back and there was not an ounce of fat on them. Our lot were flabby, breathless, flushed and their facial features were so blurred they might as well have been wearing stocking masks.

'Wouldn't like to meet any of them on a dark night,' said Dad, and the others guffawed. Because, of course, these men were the night-fighter pilots who had tried and often succeeded in shooting them down.

One by one, they introduced themselves.

'Von Beansegg!'

'Von Hamindorf!'

'Zur Buschinfelde!'

The German pilots reached forward and though they did not click their heels and though there was no trace of duelling scars on their cheeks, the British visitors felt quietly satisfied that they had conformed to the cartoon image of the old enemy. One, Colonel Bubi von Kreuznach, even wore a monocle.

The table in the messroom was decked out with plastic, model aircraft. Messerschmidt 110s, Lancasters, Heinkels, Halifaxes (the kind that I used to glue together as Airfix models). A little nest of crossed German and British flags made up the centrepiece of the display. The walls were covered with black and white photographs of planes and their crew.

'This was the headquarter of fighter squadron 300,' said Colonel Bubi. 'We pioneered the tactics of the Wilde Sau, the so-called Wild Pig – flying into the night, without guidance from below, using our naked eyes and the glare of the searchlights to shoot you down.'

'I like that,' whispered Dad, 'no nonsense about being pleased to see us.'

'One of our first missions was in July 1943 over Cologne, the city you are now visiting. Nine of us, including me, shot down twelve of your bombers. It was very satisfactory. Now I would like to wish you a very pleasant stay. And please enjoy the beef, which is from the very best German herds.'

There was a ripple of polite laughter.

'Bit abrupt,' said the parachute officer. 'Just as well, I suppose, stomach is rumbling like a washing machine.'

I sensed, though, that there was more at work than the colonel's sensitivity towards the digestive juices of the British.

'What's up with the colonel?' I asked one of the German pilots. His name tag said: Borstig. 'Is he always like this?'

'Everything is in order, I think,' said Borstig, who had the narrow chest and slight build of a fighter pilot. Some kind of pea soup with sausage had been put in front of us, in chipped white tureens marked with the crest of the unit. Borstig grimaced. He was obviously not a soup man. 'Actually, it is more complicated, I think.'

'Tell me.'

'But you are a journalist, I think.'

'Yes, that's why I'm here. But it's OK. I don't bite.'

'Before you came, we had the old argument, fought the old battle.'

'Which battle is that?'

'The battle for the Knight's Cross. Some of the officers here were in a squadron in Holland. If you had good connections you could take off early and shoot down the bombers. There was almost no risk and you were on your way to a Knight's Cross. For some of the people here today, that medal was everything.'

Borstig ran his hand across his stiff white collar. 'We used to say: they have sore throats because the cross hangs round the neck. There were always rumours that after the war we would be given special estates. Some of these officers were close to curing their sore throats – and then they were sent here. They really had to learn how to fight. It was dangerous as hell. And no way to get a medal.'

'Must have been difficult flying blind.'

'We got shot down by our own flak. Or we shot our planes by accident.'

'So some people here hate the colonel?'

'And some love him. It is as in life.'

'Why did the haters turn up?'

'The Defence ministry pays a special attendance fee for reunification meetings.'

'Sounds like Germans should be trying to reconcile themselves with Germans.'

'That, young man, is the tragedy of my country.'

'What have you been blabbing on about?' Dad was demanding attention.

'Major Borstig says you should eat your carrots. He says it's good for your night vision.'

The beef had indeed arrived with carrots. The dish was a steaming, succulent delight, eliminating at a stroke the British prejudices about German cooking.

Even Tom was briefly silenced. This was a mercy. He had spent twenty minutes telling his German hosts about his brilliant piloting skills. The British delegation, knowing full well that Tom was a back-of-the-bus man, started to cringe. Neither Tom nor my father was a great hero. A third surviving member of the crew had told me how they bailed out too early. There had been a chance to save the plane. As they floated to earth – trapped in the glare of the searchlights, waiting to be shot at – they each soiled their pants.

'Never been so frightened in my life,' my dad admitted later.

Only Tom continued to boast about his wartime career. Sixty years on, the stories had grown and mutated and lost all contact with reality.

The British tucked into second helpings and soaked up the Rhine wine. The Germans politely declined.

'God, no wonder they're so fit,' said one of the RAF men.

'That's because they were used sensibly after the war,' said Dad. 'They were given real jobs – not just dumped like we were. No wonder we let ourselves go to seed.'

A smartly-dressed man close to the head of the table coughed. It was the kind of sound you give in England when the doctor holds your balls and says 'cough!' to test if you have a hernia. An abrupt piece of social punctuation. He scraped back his chair and stood up. I had not noticed him before but that very fact told me precisely who he was: a minder from the Ministry of Information, which was keeping a wary eye on the great kiss-and-make-up operation. There was still a nervousness about letting soldiers meet. The minder was in his thirties and there wasn't – in contrast to the British guests – a crease or crinkle to be seen. His suit was smooth, his shirt, his manicured hands, his tightly suntanned face. It was as if a giant steam-iron had been applied over his whole body.

'If I might just say a few words on behalf of the German government,' he said and reached inside his jacket for his notes. I could see that none of the airmen, neither the German nor British, could stand him, or his American-accented English.

I took a paper napkin and wrote on top: IMPORTANT SPEECH. The crease-free bureaucrat noticed the gesture and smiled approvingly. The press was paying attention. As he meandered on and on, I drew up a table that seemed to represent my options:

CLAUDIA	+	-	RENATA	+	-
Ready for a fight	X		Guerrilla	X	
Likes fitness centres		X	Dislikes sport	X	
Smoker (like me)	X		Bites nails		X
Flashy car	X		Bike		X
Doesn't laugh		X	Laughs like a mule	X	
Sinewy thighs	X		Green eyes	X	

I chewed the end of my pencil. Perhaps, in the end, it was the eyes that mattered most.

The smooth bureaucrat was smoothly progressing through his speech. A few polished clichés rolled towards me, like glass marbles in a children's game. Unification, he was saying, was the end of a process and the beginning of a process. Germans could be proud again. I could see Tom was growing restless. The man was on point six. I could see on his notes, six out of ten.

The colonel, barely able to conceal his impatience, tapped his glass with a spoon.

'Thank you, that was fascinating,' he said to Herr No-Crease, blundering into the middle of a sentence. 'But the time has come, I think, for a toast.'

He sprang to his feet.

'I would like to raise my glass to the Queen!'

'To the Queen!'

Dad looked flustered. 'What's the German president's name again?'

'Köhler,' I prompted.

He rose. 'To President, er, Killer.'

The British pilots echoed: 'To Killer.'

The German colonel was up again.

'To the great fliers of the Royal Air Force.'

'Who contributed so much to the urban planning of your cities,' interjected Tom. A chilly silence fell round the table. 'Ha, ha!' Tom looked round for approval.

'My mother was killed in the Brunswick raid,' said Borstig.

'And mine in Dresden,' said another officer.

'Just a little joke,' said Tom, not at all abashed, and hissed loudly, as if on stage, 'You see – no sense of humour.'

It was beginning to resemble a lunch in Hell.

'Excuse me for a moment,' I said.

I left the room and went towards the toilets. Earlier I had noticed automatic fire sprinklers set in the ceilings, a sensible precaution on an air base with highly-explosive kerosine scattered round the academy. I lit up a Marlboro Light, stood on a chair and waited for the alarm system to work. Sure enough, bells started to ring and sirens started to howl. Water gushed out of every sprinkler.

'My God, it's an air raid,' shouted Tom, 'everyone into the bunker.'

Grimly, a clutch of British and German pilots emerged soaking from the building as if they had just been fished out of the Atlantic. The parachuter had grabbed a bottle of wine and taken shelter under the dining table. I hid the stub of my cigarette in the pot of a rubber plant.

'Perhaps we had just better move on with the next part of the programme and forget the spontaneous conversation bit.' I gently suggested to Kreuznach.

The colonel nodded. Across the camp, fire engines were hurtling towards the building. Soldiers were shouting. Aircraft were being moved into hangars.

'Any casualties?' yelled a medical team carrying breathing equipment on a stretcher. 'If you're uninjured, move as far away from the building as possible.'

'How many anti-smoke masks do we need?'

And, the most intelligent appeal of all: 'Where's the fire?'

'Could be terrorists,' said Dad, looking on the bright side of things. 'There could be anthrax in there.'

'I don't think so somehow,' said the colonel, looking straight into my eyes. I tried to avoid his gaze. Out of the window I could see a fire engine unwinding a hosepipe for the non-existent fire.

'You have a very competent rescue service, Colonel,' I said.

'And you, Sir, also have a talent for rescue.' He paused between each word to make quite clear that he was deploying irony.

'No, no, you don't understand,' chirped my father, 'he simply has a talent for catastrophe.'

'Oh, shut up, Dad.' It had been another long day.

Chapter Eleven

The Naked Truth

The apartment was as hot as a bakery, the air as thick as dough. It was the beginning of October and still the sun beat down on Berlin, making a nonsense out of the seasons. Global warming was messing up our lives.

As an Englishman I was used to a short summer, clouds fogging up the morning, then an apologetic sun appearing at about noon. For how long? Four weeks, five weeks? Then it was back to the drizzle. That was more or less the Rhineland model also, but in Berlin suddenly different meteorological rules were being set.

Oyster bars were springing up across the city. The new climate had warmed up the North Sea to such a degree that oysters were breeding like crazy, underwater rabbits. So oysters, once the food of the rich, were becoming accessible to the poor, an essential part of the diet on the dole along with salads made from dandelion leaves harvested from the overgrown car park outside the job centre. Meanwhile cod – the essential component of fish and chips, the traditional nourishment of the British working classes – was becoming a luxury. The waters of the North Sea were too warm for the fish. The world was being turned upsidedown, the seasons jumbled or abolished. What was a man to do?

Open the windows and the flies fly in, runs an old blues refrain, *close the windows and you're sweating again*.

It was time to get out of town. Berlin was getting too hot, and not only on the thermometer.

My credit cards were at that stage when a saleswoman feels it necessary to look you in the eyes, then turn her back and conduct a whispered conversation with someone on the other end of a secret phone line. After fifteen minutes of checking and counter-checking she returns and says: 'The bank accepts the payment – exceptionally.'

A letter from the bank had made the situation even more critical. A certain Frau Knete, it said ominously, would be ringing on Tuesday to discuss – urgently – the state of my finances.

Claudia had left a message saying we had to talk – urgently – and that she would be visiting me on Tuesday.

Dad and Tom had disappeared on a tour of Rhineland vineyards. They would be returning to Berlin on Tuesday.

Today was Tuesday. It seemed like a very good time to escape from the city.

Renata had made no contact. By the perverse laws of courtship, this made her more interesting.

'You're at the road-testing stage,' said Harry. 'You like the look of her. Now you have to know how the engine works. She's smart but, you know, is she a Smart?'

Harry was referring to a widely mocked model of Mercedes which had been designed to look like the kind of electric razor that women use to shave their legs. It had notoriously failed its first road test.

'You mean, find out whether she can negotiate corners on a wet road? That kind of thing?'

Harry nodded enthusiastically. 'Exactly! I can see you are getting the hang of the woman-thing.'

I had not thought of women in quite these mechanistic terms, perhaps because I was such a bad car driver. Life would have been simpler if I could have just rung up Renata and proposed that she climb into my sleek, lightning-blue, open-top sports car for a quick trip into the country.

Instead, the preparations were more elaborate.

Wednesday was German unity day, one of the founding moments of the nation. As a result nobody worked on that day, or indeed on any of the days that connected it with the weekend. The Germans called this stolen time 'bridge days', but it was sometimes difficult to see, even in a country proud of its engineering talents, how a bridge could be long and strong enough to support so many idle people.

In any case, an escape from Berlin during an extended holiday was difficult to organise, since trains were booked out – I was briefly sad about not having a flashy, fast car – and hotels too. Swatting away mosquitoes, making dozens of phone calls, applying more energy than I did to my work, I found a hotel on the Baltic Sea that would take me, a woman and a dog, and not ask embarrassing questions about my creditworthiness. Only when all the pieces were in place did I call Renata.

'Er, hello,' I said, feeling strangely shy when I eventually rang.

'Oh, it's you.' Her voice was warm, perhaps with the memory of a kiss, our snatched moment.

'I wondered whether you would like to go to the seaside for a day or two, get out of town.' I deliberately used the English word 'seaside': it smacked of child-like innocence. 'Just a spontaneous thing,' I lied. 'Would do us both good.'

'The Baltic?' She sounded hesitant. 'I will be up there anyway in Rostock, but I don't know.'

'Come on. It will do you good. You can pamper yourself at the spa.'

I could almost hear her thinking: do I want to enter a fully-fledged relationship with this man? How close have we become? How much intimacy could our relationship sustain?

'I've booked a room with a view,' I said jauntily but I wanted to convey the message: a room with a double bed.

'How have you been?' she asked suddenly.

I guessed she was buying time. There was an ethical decision to be made.

'I've been thinking about you,' I said. That was true. I had been pre-occupied with Renata much more than Claudia and sometimes I feared that the relationship was entirely in my head.

'Me too.' A pause. 'All right, I'll come.'

'Yes!' I hissed to myself, as if my team had just scored a decisive goal.

'What was that noise?' she asked.

'The kettle,' I said.

We agreed that we would travel separately to Heiligendamm. Renata was designing a monument for German refugees who had drowned in the Baltic; she would drive from Rostock. I, carless, would come up by train.

And a very unpleasant journey it was too. Travel before German holidays always resembled a scramble for the lifeboats. Hordes of shoppers stripped the shelves of supermarkets, grumbling at the slow-thinking cashier, cash machines ran dry and rubbish collectors decided it would be folly to clean the railway stations because holiday makers would just spoil their work.

On the train, forty-five minutes late (due to 'technical disturbances'), the gangways were bursting with squabbling teenagers and tipsy soldiers who had twenty-four hours leave from the barracks. And the toilet was blocked not by the usual suspects – tampons and dropped mobile phones – but by a man's shoe, size forty-three.

'There's a shoe in your toilet,' I told the ticket inspector as he strode down the aisles.

German ticket inspectors have gone through a strange evolution. In the 1980s they looked profoundly uncomfortable, as if they were conscientious objectors forced into uniform. By the 1990s they were sporting little beards and gold-rimmed glasses, in sympathy, it seemed, with the leadership of the Social Democrats. Then came the gay phase: earrings, gelled hair, a slight wiggle of the hips. Now they had a more military air about them, though they resembled corrupt regimental quartermasters rather than fighting men.

'Not my responsibility,' he said, 'if you are unhappy, send a letter to our service team in Frankfurt.'

'But it's your train,' I said, 'and your toilet, and there's a man somewhere walking round without a shoe.' I corrected myself. 'Or rather, with one shoe.'

I could see his eyes glaze over as if part of some ceramic manufacturing process.

'Size forty-three,' I said, helpfully.

'Can I ask you a question, Sir?' he said, and without asking for an answer, continued, 'Do you work in an office? And do you clean the toilets in that office? I bet you don't. Well, nor do I. Now if you will excuse me... '

The man started to prance down the train. Perhaps I was in an unusually excitable frame of mind, because of my approaching rendezvous. Whatever the reason, I ran after him.

'Look, maybe someone tried to kill himself. And got his foot stuck in the toilet.'

I had to admit it did not seem very plausible.

'I mean, you're responsible for the safety of your passengers, aren't you? Or do you just punch holes in tickets?'

Plainly I had touched a nerve. The man's puffy face was turning lobster-red. I definitely preferred it when inspectors looked gay.

'If you have reason to believe that someone may have killed himself, the correct behaviour is to pull the emergency lever. The train will stop. If the authorities believe you have made a frivolous decision, you are liable to a fine of fifteen-hundred euros. In some circumstances you can be imprisoned.'

Lobster-face and I stared eye to eye.

'The person who decides whether the emergency stop is justified or not, is the senior inspector,' he said, with menace. 'And I am that man.'

'Right,' I said, and sat down in my seat next to Mac who was being unusually patient. On the whole he disliked men in uniform. 'Right,' I said again. 'Point taken. Might is right. I just wanted to inform you of a deficiency in your train.'

I had lost the urge for an argument. This was the day that I was to lay siege to Renata and I needed to save my energy.

Just at that moment the train rattled to a halt. Through the windows I could see the golden fields of Mecklenburg. The sun caught a farmer on a tractor who shielded his eyes to look at the stalled train.

The inspector glared at me as if suspecting that I had secretly pulled the emergency brake. I raised my hands as if weighing coconuts, a theatrical shrug.

'Not me,' I said, and gave him my most provocative smile. The inspector's mobile rang and he disappeared, looking suddenly very important.

There followed a long pause, maybe twenty minutes. I hoped that Renata wasn't waiting at the station. We had agreed to meet in the hotel but she might have been the kind of woman who likes to gather in her flock, a shepherdess.

The passengers were growing restless. An old man, overdressed like all pensioners in a waistcoat and tweed jacket, shuffled to the end of the carriage to gulp some fresh air.

Mac and I joined him. Outside there was a huge and birdless silence.

'Don't open the doors!' barked the inspector who appeared from behind.

'No need to shout,' I said. 'Why are we not moving?'

'I am about to make an announcement.'

'Well, perhaps, you could tell us now since you're standing in front of us,' I said. 'This gentleman is not feeling very well.'

Indeed, the old man was sweating. 'Could the delay have something to do with the shoe blocked in the toilet?'

'Of course not,' snapped the railway official. 'A suitcase has been found abandoned on the tracks.' The German phrase was a *'herrenloser koffer'* – a case without a master.

I started to laugh. Did all suitcases in Germany need a master?

The official took a step towards me. He probably had just briefly lost his balance although, since the train was stalled it was difficult to see how this could have happened. It was plain that he did not like my laughter. Dogs, on the other hand, do not like ambiguous movement. Mac growled, bared his teeth and in a burst of energy reminiscent of the launch of a V2 rocket, he bit into the crotch of the inspector.

No, it was not a very successful journey.

The inspector, surprisingly, became a nicer man after switching roles from bully to victim. Perhaps he sensed that he was about to be generously compensated by my insurance company. Whatever the reason he sat calmly on a luggage cart in Rostock station, cradling his testicles, enjoying the sun and awaiting the arrival of medical staff.

A sheepish Mac, shouted at and disciplined, cowered nearby while the old man explained to me the story of the shoe. He had been so over-heated in the train that he had gone to the toilet to wash his feet in the sink and thus reduce the risk of swelling and thrombosis. One of the shoes had slipped and jammed in the toilet. But even the solution of a mystery – the missing shoe belonged to the disorientated old man – could not disguise the fact that the little holiday on the Baltic had started badly.

It was good to arrive at last in the Heiligendamm hotel complex. The steady buzz of machines vacuuming up unsightly leaves reminded me of my well-ordered boarding school where more attention was paid to the condition of the cricket pitches than to the health of its pupils. It was institutional gardening, the kind that is supposed to make a political point: Welcome to our parade ground, it seemed to say, everything is neat and in its place, make sure you behave accordingly. The white houses were built in the early nineteenth century, but the true Heiligendamm was best seen in the slightly decaying seaside villas that fringed the hotel. Wooden shutters banged as a sea breeze spoiled non-gelled hairstyles and fluttered the flags, including an upside down Union Jack.

The dog, still not quite forgiven for his attitude towards German Rail, cocked his ears and raised his twitching nose. It was a positive sign: Mac, like me, was a fan of the Baltic. Perhaps, just perhaps, a messy day of flight from my problems could be gently resolved.

I realised that I was looking forward to seeing Renata; since Becky's departure, the rhythm of life had been mainly dictated by work and by male friendship and by brief expeditions to Planet Woman. The need for a tax spouse had masked a real emotional need for female companionship. Could Renata offer me that? Or was she too brittle?

The spa receptionist told me that Renata was in the seaweed treatment room but Mac could not accompany me since algae were, apparently, allergic to dog hair. I tethered him to the receptionist's chair and promised him a posh hairdo and Reiki massage just as soon as we were back in Berlin. It did not seem to improve his mood but there were limits, as Tony kept telling me, as to how guilty a man could be made to feel by a dog or indeed a woman.

The treatment room was empty. There was a half drunken bottle of algae wine – Chateau Seaweed – and two glasses so it looked as if Renata and the cosmetician had been having a good time. Next to the mirror, lit up with little light bulbs like the changing room of a lead actress, there were pots of ointments and face creams and jellies.

And an open handbag.

For twenty-three seconds – the time it took to check that Renata was not hiding behind the shower curtain – I wrestled with my conscience. A woman's handbag is the ultimate temptation for a man, the key to understanding. If I had been a private detective I would not have hesitated and it seemed to me that journalists are the Miss Marples of the modern age.

At first the haul was disappointing: Chanel lipstick and gloss might have hinted at an intention to kiss; a little mirror suggested more vanity than I had anticipated. The packet of Petibelle contraceptive pills indicated that she was reaching the end of her menstrual cycle. A number scrawled on the back of a crumpled *Othello* programme was, I realised, my mobile phone.

I was about to start reading her diary when I heard a gruff voice:

'Big Mother is watching you!'

I spun round to see something resembling a Pharaonic mummy escaping from the tomb, wrapped in green bandages from head to foot, only the eyes and mouth open to view.

'You are a very curious man,' said the voice and it was, of course, Renata.

I let the diary slip back into the handbag.

'My God, Renata, you scared the wits out of me. You look like a giant piece of sushi.'

'Smell like one, more like it. You should try being wrapped in seaweed.'

'No, thanks,' I said, and looked more carefully at her.

The seaweed infused bandages were strapped highly round her legs, emphasising their slimness. I wondered if she had seen me rifling through her bag.

'When will you get out of your bodywrap?'

'Another ninety minutes,' she said. 'Why don't you go to the sea and get some air. You look a bit jaded.'

'Difficult trip,' I said. 'I'll take the dog on the dunes.'

I made as if to kiss her but she shied away.

'Don't be ridiculous, I look like a zombie.'

This was true.

As I left I saw her walk, with stiff movements, towards her handbag. Had she seen me fiddling round? If so, another negative point had been notched up; my luck had still not turned.

At the reception desk I bought a copy of *Bunte*, a glossy magazine which serves as the official house organ of the various hairdressers, talk-show hosts and Eurovision song-writers who secretly run this country, and a bar of tooth-rotting chocolate which I intended to share with Mac in the sun.

It was the most self-indulgent gesture I could think of, a reward for a crappy day.

The dog and I wandered across the cliffs, past more crumbling houses, then down a steep path towards the sea.

It was here that some eighteenth-century Duke of Mecklenburg-Schwerin had been told to bathe by his doctor, probably to cure a sexual disease with seawater, algae and sun.

Nowadays German aristocrats suffered from the same ailments but preferred to treat them with antibiotics and a trip to the Caribbean.

Ever since childhood the sea had been an escape for me. Other children dreamed of running away with a circus but I could never understand that: the permanent smell of elephant shit was a high price to pay for freedom from your parents. But disappearing on a banana boat to South America, that had real appeal. The howl of the wind, the salt on the lips. My first encounters with boats, however, had been less than successful. One choppy trip across the North Sea with my grandmother stuck in the memory. She was sick and lost her false teeth in the lavatory bowl. Then I was sick and lost my favourite fountain pen, which slipped out of the top pocket of my school blazer and fell into the sea where it was no doubt swallowed by herrings. So my love of the sea was confined to the beach and the cliffs, to watching the horizon, to narrowing my eyes and trying to make out the shape of distant container ships.

As I made my way from the hotel to the craggy beaches, the old sense of liberation returned. Yes, there were huge problems piling up – the money, the future of my father – but proximity to the sea persuaded me that somehow I could solve them. Would it be so bad if I married somebody like Renata? I genuinely liked her and I think the feeling was mutual. Perhaps there would be more. Did it matter, in the end, if as a by-product, I also cut my tax bill and helped out my dad? I felt sure my father would like her – he would be scared by Claudia, all those muscles and cigarettes and the political passion. But, of course, both women were German and that would be a big psychological leap for my father.

The dog, his lungs pumped full of ozone, cantered ahead like an Indian scout. The sand rose up, as smooth and crisp as a ski slope and I lost sight of him. Whistling for Mac, I plodded up the incline, wishing I was wearing Birkenstocks. When I reached the top, sweating, cursing the animal and fingering the melted chocolate in my pocket, I found myself on a sand-crest.

Down below I could see a cove, hidden from view, protected by a wall of dunes. It was quite magical; I felt like Leonardo DiCaprio in *The Beach*, at the doorstep of a clandestine world. Straining my eyes against the glare of the sun I could make out Mac gambolling between what looked like dozens of stranded porpoises.

'You are in a clothes-free zone,' barked a woman, approaching from my left side.

And sure enough she was wearing nothing but silicone artfully tucked into her naked breasts. Every part of her torso wobbled apart from those breasts which remained as stable and as solid as the twin hulls of a catamaran.

This was not, I sensed immediately, a woman to be crossed.

'I've lost my dog,' I said, waving my hand towards the beach below. The porpoises I realised were naked humans. 'I need to get him back.'

'Well, then you have to take your clothes off,' said the woman crisply. 'This is a FKK beach.' The initials stood for *Freie Körper Kultur* – Free Body Culture. Nudies, in other words.

'It's not possible to be clothed on a nudist beach?'

The woman in her late thirties, her eyes crinkled from sunbathing, looked at me as if I were a pervert.

'We wouldn't be nudists any more then, would we?' she said in a grating accent that could only come from the Ruhr.

I should have guessed: a West German!

The strict no-clothes rules of FKK, the dogma of nudity, were upheld by the Wessis, the West Germans.

The Ossis, the East Germans, had actually fought for their right to nakedness and were therefore more flexible. The Baltic nudists in communist days (in the 1950s at least) were intellectuals who were mimicking the sun-worshipping tradition of the German Workers' Movement.

The regime hated it all (they were self-loathing prudes). Police tried to arrest the naked protestors who managed to dodge the restriction by organising 'Cameroon festivals' celebrating the socialist brotherhood between the DDR and the African country. Just an excuse, of course, for hundreds to dance naked on the sand.

For Ossis nudity was about tolerance; for Wessis it was about rule enforcement.

'Can't I keep on some shorts, at least?' I said. 'Look how pale I am. I could get skin cancer. I just want to get the dog back. Unless... ' – the solution was obvious – 'you could rustle up a team to catch him and bring him to me. He's only little.' I held out the lead.

'The dog is your responsibility, not ours.'

I tried whistling again to see if Mac would return of his own free will. But he was having too good a time, smelling human penises and splashing in the waves.

'Mac!' I shouted in a sharp, barrack-room voice. 'It's no good,' I said turning to the FKK sentinel.

Wordlessly she held her arms out in front of her. I reluctantly took off my shoes, my shirt and trousers and handed them over.

'Shorts too?'

'Shorts too.'

'What if I get sunburn?' The sun was indeed beating down strongly for October.

'We have creams. And we use seaweed.'

'What, even down there?' I blenched.

The boxer shorts joined the pile. Together we made our way down to the cove. *Bunte* covered my private parts. Thank God for *Bunte*.

I am blonde, but a British blonde. It is difficult to believe in a blonde master race if you turn the colour and consistency of wet clay after half-an-hour in the sun. Long before skin cancer became the standard summer catastrophe alert, I was being instructed by an over-anxious mother (Dad was usually in a shady pub) to wear floppy hats and long-sleeved shirts to shield my chicken-white body from the feeble rays of the British sun.

Blondes really are destined for leadership. You don't have to be a Nazi to see that, just an alert, intelligent reader.

Blondes, not redheads, or brunettes, are the stuff of fairy tales.

The Greeks had a word for it, *xanthos*, which suggested not only blondeness but also yellow, gold-yellow, touched by light. Homer made Achilles blonde, and his horse too. Mary, the mother of Jesus, is a Renaissance blonde, as is her son. But blonde and pale – in an age where pallor is associated with disease – sends confusing signals.

So the FKK beach was full of deep-tanned blondes: Germans obviously placed a high priority on consistency. The FKK legion wanted to be clearly identified as winners – blonde hair follicles and brown bodies.

And yet deception, I realised, was at the heart of the German naturist movement. Either they were blonded by hydrogen peroxide or browned by fake-bake. Or both.

My plan was to half close my eyes – if I can't see them, they can't see me – thread my way through the bodies, grab my bloody dog, reclaim my clothes and make a quick exit. The key was anonymity.

Just imagine, I said to myself, that you are fully clothed in the crowded London Underground, surrounded by people avoiding each other's eyes. You learn, as a Londoner, to avoid body contact, to remove yourself from the heavy breathing, the sweating and the farting by a process of transcendental meditation: commuter yoga.

The same process can surely be applied to a nudist beach.

'Hello! My friend!'

A confident baritone penetrated the contemplative silence of the sunbathers. Everybody looked up, curiously, at the English intruder.

I shaded my eyes with one hand, the other resolutely holding my strategic *Bunte*.

It was – my heart sank – Ruediger. Looking, of course, very fit, with a smooth, obviously shaven, chest. And regulation blonde-brown.

'Friends,' he said loudly, ensuring that the population of the beach, perhaps sixty people, held their gaze on my body, 'this is a very prominent British journalist.'

'Thanks, Ruediger,' I said through gritted teeth, 'perhaps you would like to hand out my mobile phone number.'

'Come and sit with us. Forget your dog, he's having a good time.'

Mac was indeed enjoying himself, sniffing at women like a dog trained to track down botox and silicone.

I looked at my watch. There was still an hour to go before Renata would be finished with her seaweed. I then realised that I had removed my fig-leaf.

'OK, I suppose so,' I said grudgingly, realising it was better to lie down naked than stand up.

The beach was divided on East-West lines, with the Ossis starting to grill some Thueringer Wurst and throw balls at each other, and the Wessis listening to iPods.

Ruediger was naturally on the Western side, along with a much younger girlfriend. I noted with approval that she was blonde on top, dark Brazilian between her legs and rosy-pale in between. She slowly took off her Chanel sunglasses and glared at me, as if to say: don't let your eyes stray.

'Darling, this man almost beat me at the marathon.' Ruediger could barely conceal his resentment.

'Let myself go a bit since then,' I said apologetically. Some rational explanation had to be found for the marked difference in physical shape between Ruediger and myself. 'Anyway, you know, it's not the winning that counts. It's a question of conquering the flesh.'

'Playing the game,' said Ruediger, in English, 'is everything.'

I looked more closely at Ruediger's companion or at least at her face. It was obviously taboo to study anything else. Big eyes, upturned nose, sensual lips.

'A short break together?'

The girl nodded.

'Yeah, the day of German unity,' she said. We both laughed.

'What's so funny about that,' said Ruediger, worried that he had missed something, that control of the conversation was slipping away from him. Then, just to show that he had a cracking sense of humour, he flashed his teeth, as white as a lavatory cistern. No one could accuse Ruediger of being laid back. But, to his credit, there was not a single flaw on his body. He was hairless, oiled, muscled, as sleek as an otter. Plainly the girl liked her men well-plucked.

'What's your name?' I asked, since Ruediger had not bothered to introduce the girl. She was, it seemed, a fashion accessory.

'Rose,' she said and I caught the hint of an English accent.

'You're English?'

She nodded. Rose did not seem to speak very much.

'Rose is *very* English,' said Ruediger. 'We have packed a five o'clock afternoon tea in our picnic basket.'

He pointed at a pannier big enough to house a week's rations. A vacuum flask peeked out of the cover, as did the edge of a checked tablecloth.

'I hope,' added Ruediger, 'you will join us for cucumber sandwiches. We like to do things the English way.'

'I think you will find, Ruediger, that the English don't take their afternoon tea naked,' I said.

'No matter. We have all the ingredients needed for a good cocktail too. I could make you Sex on the Beach, no, Rose?'

Rose rolled her eyes in my direction.

'That's the name of a cocktail, you understand. Just my little double entendre.'

'Yes, I think I got that,' I said, and looked at my watch.

Soon it would be time to collect Renata. But suddenly, despite the manifest absurdity of the situation – Ruediger's clunking style, the compulsory nudity – I was surprisingly happy to stay where I was.

'Do you work at the Deutsche Bank, like Ruediger?'

Ruediger was determined that his girlfriend should not be allowed to speak for herself.

'No, Rose is creative,' he said.

'Oh really, what… ?' Before I could complete the sentence I felt an excruciating pain on the end of my naked cock. It was as if a stiletto had been stubbed into a nerve ending. *Aedans vexans*, the plague of that summer, had struck again.

'Oh, shit!'

The skin is thin down there and, if caught by the sun, very sensitive. The foreskin was beginning to swell and redden.

'Get some ice, Ruediger,' said Rose, taking command. He reached inside the picnic hamper and rummaged among the cocktail-making equipment. Rose broke off about eight ice cubes and rolled them into a towel which she dampened with Evian water.

'Here!' she said, handing me the improvised compress while trying to avert her eyes from the injured organ. It felt good.

'Keep pressing,' she said.

'How do you know these things?'

'Grew up on a farm,' she said, 'once you've milked a few cows, you know how to deal with sore udders.'

She flashed a smile and displayed a set of small, neat teeth, not gravestone perfect like Ruediger's, but as charming as a pearl necklace.

Mac, sensing commotion, had come over to join us.

'A fine English dog, I think,' said Ruediger.

'Scottish.'

'A hunting dog, no doubt.'

'Only rats,' I said, just as Mac started to paw at the picnic hamper. He could smell cold chicken and was determined to snatch himself a leg or a breast.

'Stop it!' I barked.

Mac ignored me and started to nudge the basket with his nose in an attempt to spill its contents. I could see Ruediger becoming irritated. It was, after all, almost five o'clock, time for tea.

I reached over to pull the dog's snout out of the food. The compress fell off as I made the uncoordinated lunge towards the basket.

'Keep the ice in place!' exclaimed Rose and gathered up the towel. With the practised reflexes of a nurse, or indeed a helper on the family farm, she pressed the ice back onto my crotch.

'Oh, that's good,' I said. And it was.

'Oh, is it?' That was Renata. She had appeared suddenly at our side. 'Just exactly how good?'

Rose, her hand still on my crotch performing its emergency medicine, and I looked up to see a clearly furious woman. I noticed an endearing piece of seaweed still stuck to Renata's clear forehead.

'Don't get the wrong end of the stick, Renata,' I gabbled. 'I can explain everything.'

'I am sure you can. Exactly how many girlfriends do you have?'

'This is Rose,' I said, 'She was just helping out. Bit of a crisis.'

Renata's face was changing colour before my eyes, swelling with anger. All I could think of, however, was the inconsistency, the breakdown of logic.

'You've got your clothes on,' I said to Renata.

'Evidently.'

'But that's not allowed.' And indeed the FKK sentinel who had forced me to strip was standing nearby, watching the scene, hands on bulging hips, getting ready to read out the rules and expel Renata from Paradise.

'Don't be so bloody German,' Renata shouted at me and then turned on her heel.

'Seems you have trouble,' said Rose, who did not appear very upset at the prospect.

'I don't think I need much more of that, thanks,' I told her, gently removing her hand from the compress.

'So you won't be staying for tea?' asked Ruediger redundantly.

I tipped the sand out of my shoes and started to search for my clothes. Out of the corner I saw Mac discreetly pissing on Ruediger's picnic. The day could not get any worse.

Chapter Twelve

Dinner For Three

'Do you think I look fat?'

It was Rose and she looked anything but dumpy. The question, however, was directed at Ruediger so I knew the answer would not be destined to boost his girlfriend's self esteem.

'Would I be together with you if you were fat?'

'No, I suppose not,' said Rose, obviously trying to puzzle out if this was supposed to be a compliment.

'Well, there's your answer, you silly little thing. Just make sure not to eat too much for dinner.'

Rose blenched. I grimaced.

'Just a little joke,' guffawed Ruediger, failing to notice the pained silence. 'Ha, ha!'

'Ha, ha,' said Rose, flatly.

'Yes, ha, ha,' I muttered.

We were standing together, Rose and Ruediger, Renata and I, waiting to be placed in the dining room.

As soon as Renata glimpsed Rose she had hissed at me: 'I do *not* want to be at the same table as that English siren!' Since Renata's angry exit from the FKK beach I had devoted two hours of reassurance and flattery to soothing her nerves. We sat on the kingsize bed, the sea just about visible if you crooked your neck, while I tried to explain that I was not a galavanting playboy who picked up women on speed dates and then immediately betrayed them on the beach.

'Look at me,' I said. 'Do I wear a gold chain? Do I wear cut-away shirts that show off matted chest hair?'

'No, but you lie naked next to strange women and allow them to cradle your crotch. I hadn't even seen you naked and I am supposed to be in a relationship with you! And an English woman too. They're such tramps!'

'I wouldn't say that.' Were we in a relationship? She thought so...

I remembered one early attempt to kiss an English girl. I was seventeen, even clumsier than now, and lurched at her. The girl had rebuffed me with a prissy:

'I'd rather not, if it's all the same to you.'

It was the same phrase used to decline a cup of tea. No, English girls were not synonymous with passion.

'They make very good nurses,' I told Renata but was aware that I wasn't telling the whole story.

The brief encounter with Rose had reminded me of the essential difference between the English and the Germans: a lightness of being. All the stress that had been piling up on over the past weeks had masked a fundamental truth – that love was supposed to be fun. Overload it with expectations and duties, box it in with careful phrasing and sensitive gestures, and sooner or later it buckles under the strain.

We kissed, Renata and I, before heading towards the dining room but it was a cautious act. There was a stiffness to her, a remoteness. I was on probation.

'Let's eat,' she said, standing up briskly.

Meaning: perhaps sitting together over good food will take away the tension.

While Renata applied make-up in the bathroom, I stretched out on the bed and read my horoscope in *Bunte*. Grains of sand fell from between the paper and onto the sheets. Some of the pages had stuck together from the combination of ice and cooling sun lotion that had been applied to my (still sore) organ in the afternoon mosquito crisis. The horoscopes, fortunately, could still be read.

LEO (23.7. – 23.8.)
Do not overdo sporting activity, warns the Sun (your source of vitality) even if the weather is tempting.

Well, there was no chance of that. Sport had been off the agenda since the marathon.

Jupiter creates a disturbance field that makes you impatient; nothing can go fast enough for you. Those round you do not have it easy with you.

Bloody Jupiter. The horoscope continued in this vein. I had to make a painful choice. I was going to be unpopular; money was going to be a problem. Mercury was ignoring me again.

Then came the killer phrase: *This week's most unfortunate star sign*.

I could not remember Renata's star sign though it had been on the speed-dating form. Should I ask her or would it be interpreted as a further sign of neglect?

From inside the bathroom I could hear the clatter of perfume bottles and electric toothbrushes being unpacked and laid out on one side of the sink. It was always a strange moment: sharing space before you had made love. The bathroom was such an intimate zone yet we were in a pre-intimate phase.

Could it, I wondered, work out between us, become a natural relationship even if it was based on an unnatural premise?

I decided it would be tactless to ask her birth date.

Claudia, I remembered, was an Aquarian, a *dangerous* Aquarian. She had been leaving messages ever since the marathon and, to my lasting discredit, I had not returned them. Claudia obviously wanted clarity but that was the very last thing I could offer at the moment. I needed to know whether it would work out with Renata. If it flopped with her – and the omens had not been good all day – then, well, perhaps one could make a go of Claudia. Nobody wants to hear they are on the reserve-bench so, I figured, I was sparing her feelings, protecting her from hurt, by avoiding her until I knew what was going on.

'You're being a coward,' said Harry when I had told him about my doubts. I pleaded guilty.

'That's OK,' he said, 'that's the male condition. Women expect us to be cowards. It's how we're programmed. Now, how's the road test going?'

There was no progress report to be delivered as yet and so my disappointed guru had hung up. On my shoulders – or rather inside them, in the muscles that were so clenched I could hardly move my neck – I felt the weight of expectations. From the Inland Revenue, from the women who were supposed to solve my financial problems, even from my father who had mysteriously disappeared from view, somewhere in Germany.

AQUARIAN (21.1. – 20.2.)
Exciting times for singles in love. Love-planet Venus signals a meeting that will release a storm of emotion and which could even lead to a period of strain.

I did not read further. Why did *Bunte*, so painfully cheerful in its glossy articles, publish such depressing predictions?

'Are you ready?' called Renata from the bathroom. She sounded excited at the prospect of good food.

'I suppose so.'

'Lovers usually sound a bit more enthusiastic than that,' she said, popping her head round the door.

She was, I suspected, only half-mocking. Nonetheless, she locked her arm in mine as we walked to dinner. I thought that well, yes, perhaps, the day could end up successfully after all.

There were about eight guests waiting in the small ante-room in front of the dining room. Through the tall, glass doors we could see the high, gilded ceilings and the big French windows that opened up to the terrace and onto the sea. My nostrils flared as I caught the smell of roast duck. My stomach started to rumble loudly. I had eaten nothing since breakfast.

'I could eat a horse,' whispered Renata, leaning into me.

'You may have to. This is the East, remember,' I said in what I thought to be a spirit of conspiratorial good humour. Renata snorted, untouched. Once some food had been stuffed into Renata's stomach though, I felt sure her mood would change.

Sadly the woman in charge of handing out tables, the maitresse d'hotel, had also picked up on the conversation. Through thick lenses, she glared at me. Ruediger was giving his name to her as if announcing the winner of the Nobel prize for chemistry.

'M-a-t-u-s-s-e-k,' he said, 'and partner.'

Rose looked miserable.

'You have a reservation?'

'Of course, Suite 301. The very large one in the tower.'

'Ah yes, Herr Matussek,' said the maitresse d' in a thick Mecklenburg slur and ticked his name off the list in front of her. She grabbed her clipboard. 'Follow me.'

We watched them walk to a large central table that had been decked out with hydrangeas. The maitresse d' was in a strange mauve suit, Aeroflot stewardess circa 1986, and her heels clicked as they struck the wooden parquet. Ruediger was preening himself as usual. Twice he slid back his navy, gold-buttoned blazer to check the time, or more precisely, his Rolex Oyster. Rose, tottering behind him, looked almost like a child, her narrow frame in a tailored black trouser suit. Her hair was tied up. It seemed strange to see her with clothes on.

Aeroflot returned and searched for our reservations. Pointlessly, of course, because I had forgotten to book a table.

'Look,' I said taking Aeroflot to one side. 'We've got this special deal. Day-of-German-unity package. All inclusive, dinner too. So obviously there's a table for us. Or the whole system collapses.'

Aeroflot was not impressed.

'Dinner is not included – you are mistaken. And without a reservation it is going to be very difficult indeed.' She tutted. 'Tch. Tch. Very difficult.'

The queue behind us was growing restless.

'Perhaps if you could just let go of my arm and stand aside, Sir?'

Renata's anger was mounting. Not, as I thought initially, at the hotel's obduracy but rather at my incompetence. Her whole manner – her hands clenching and unclenching like one of those one-euro-a-go crane machines at funfairs – indicated that she would happily castrate me. Perhaps her mood was fuelled by the odd stares from the queuing diners. As they trooped past us, checked off one by one by Miss Aeroflot, they stared rather pointedly at my trousers. Most, I realised, had been on the FKK beach and were therefore curious about what had happened to my bitten penis. The atmosphere was of a happy funeral; the mourners filing past the grieving, giving shy nods of commiseration. It was, no doubt, meant kindly. For Renata, though, it was intolerable; she plainly hated to be left out of a secret.

'Why are they all looking at you?' she demanded to know. 'Have you met them before?'

At last our turn came. Renata, ever the Wessi, had suggested rolling up a five-euro note and slipping it into the hand of Miss Aeroflot – who treated the gesture with the contempt it deserved.

'I think you may have dropped this,' she said to me loudly, picking up the five-euro bill and holding it up for public view.

By way of punishment, she made us wait a further ten minutes. And by the time we were led through the dining room, I was as irritated by Renata as she was by me. We passed

Ruediger and Rose, well into their en croûte, and were exiled by Aeroflot to the restaurant Siberia. The table would have been cramped for a couple of garden gnomes. It was next to the hot, noisy kitchens. Only the draught from the constant swinging door provided relief from the heat of the ovens. On the adjacent table there was a frazzled mother struggling to control a baby and a pair of baboon-like identical twins. The view of the sea was blocked by a vast rubber plant.

'Well, this is nice, isn't it?' I said, brushing crumbs and what looked like a money spider from the tablecloth.

'Yes, isn't it,' said Renata staring at the tablecloth. 'Please don't kill the spider. They bring luck.'

Ruediger was waving his napkin as if it were a flag about to be planted on occupied territory. Why don't you join us?' he shouted, 'you have such a terrible table.'

'Over your dead body,' threatened Renata in her stage whisper.

'No, thanks, Ruediger,' I called back. We might as well have been on two ships passing in the night – mine a rubber dingy about to sink, his a whopping great yacht, the kind used by supermodels and American rappers. 'It's great here, so lively.'

The menus came in duplicate. The first was the written version which in pseudo-ancient calligraphy announced the six courses. The second was a buck-toothed, waist-coated waiter who, with one gloved hand behind his back, recited the whole menu as if it were an epic Nordic saga.

'The chef particularly recommends the red beetroot soup with sour cream in Brandenburg-style with a wonderful selection of black and white grain bread hand-ground by the bakers of the region,' he told us in one breath, the words tumbling out of his mouth before he could forget them.

'Or,' he continued, 'if you prefer Mediterranean flair, the chef has prepared a Zuppa di Gamberetti e Zucchini using cherry tomatoes hand picked from the Spree-Lausitz with...'

'That's enough, thanks,' I said firmly. 'We can read the menus ourselves, I think.'

The waiter walked away with the injured air of a Jehovah's Witness who just had a door slammed in his face.

'I'm sick of this damned service-culture,' I fumed. 'Teaching East German kids to recite dishes like parrots. Teaching them to smile, for God's sake! It's like bloody California!'

'I didn't realise you were so intolerant,' said Renata. 'I always like to have full information about what I eat.'

A process of disillusionment, I could see, was setting in. I needed to convince Renata that I was not a hopeless cynic.

'Sorry,' I said, and reached over to touch her wrist. 'I'm just very hungry.'

'Me too,' Renata replied dangerously, pushing the hand away.

I ordered a bottle of champagne and glared so hard at the wine-waiter that he did not even dare to tell me who had picked the grapes. Nearby the baby was beginning to squawk and from the kitchen came the clatter of dropped dishes. But I did not utter a word of complaint. Whining and dining was unattractive.

'So,' I said, picking up my glass and taking a huge slug. 'When were you last on the Baltic, Renata?'

'Oh... ' she paused. 'Ages ago.'

'Tell me about it.'

'No, I don't want to.'

'Come on, Renata. I know so little about you.'

This was true. Apart from the seven minutes of speed dating and our theatre excursion – the kiss! – there had been precious little information exchanged. Enough, however, to establish a mutual sympathy and a strong-enough attraction to share a kingsize bed. But little else. Renata was still a mystery.

I looked at her. She was wearing a simple v-neck dress without jewellery, her one adornment a striped silk scarf. Again and again her hands returned to the scarf, loosening it and then tightening it again. It occurred to me: she is simulating strangulation. Renata was still pent up with anger; maybe she wanted to strangle me, or herself for having been so stupid as to agree to a mini-break with me.

'Renata, you're not jealous, are you? About what happened on the beach? I mean, first, nothing happened and second, you told me at the theatre that you had conquered jealousy for ever.'

'Of course not,' she said sharply, 'why would I be jealous about a man?'

The waiter arrived with a plate of meat, or as he put it: 'A threefold delight of breast of chicken de Havelland and liver of duck specially prepared by… '

I held up my hand. His mouth slammed shut.

'We know what we ordered, thank-you very much.'

Renata was displeased but the smell of the meat deflected her anger.

'You were going to tell me about your last Baltic adventure,' I said, picking up my knife and fork.

'I really don't want to.'

'Please… '

Renata sighed and embarked on a charming family saga. At least, it was charming for a while.

Then I lost concentration and started to study her face, the fine, delicately-erotic lines that were beginning to form round her eyes.

I poured her more champagne but she had barely touched her glass. I was on my third. She was becoming captivated by her own story and there was something irresistible about the sudden animation of her face. The actual words, I sensed, were less than fascinating. Fragments drifted in my direction… bucket and spade… sandcastles… picnic on the cliffs… family arguments… the sudden, dangerous winds. I studied Renata's lips as they related the story and thought about the sensuality of narrative, how stories spun a sexual spell.

' …and that, you see, is when my brother died,' she said at last.

I sat up with a jerk. Oh God! What had I missed?

'His body was washed up on the shore.'

Renata's lips were quivering now, her eyes brimming with tears.

'That was the last time I saw him. And the last time I was on holiday on the Baltic. You can see the cliff from the hotel.'

'How terrible!' Indeed, it was. 'I'm so sorry I brought you here. Why didn't you tell me?'

'I tried… but you didn't seem to listen.'

I remembered her long hesitation, her resistance which I had interpreted as coyness or modesty.

'Anyway, my therapist told me I should confront my fears.'

A therapist? Could things get any worse? Not only was I using Renata to solve my tax problems, she was using me to solve her emotional dilemmas. I had become part of her therapy. Perhaps this was the way that modern German relationships functioned, but it left me confused.

I reached forward to touch her hand and wondered whether I should not get up, come round to her chair and hold her. I cursed inwardly. If only I had listened more intently to the story about her drowned brother.

The phone rang, interrupting my thought processes. I dug it out of my pocket.

'Sorry,' I said to Renata and then, realising that we had already become the centre of attention in the dining room, nodded a curt apology to the nearby tables.

'Can you talk?' It was Harry, his voice more urgent than usual. In the background I could hear the cacophony of street traffic.

'Not really,' I said. 'It's a bit delicate at the moment.' I looked up at Renata who was dabbing her eyes with the napkin.

'Well, get away for a second. It's important.'

'It's work,' I mouthed to Renata, pointing at the phone.

I could see the waiter approaching with more plates, ready to embark on yet another Hamletian monologue. At a sharp pace, I passed Ruediger and Rose – he was leaning towards her to say something, she was backing off as if he had halitosis – and made my way to the door.

'OK now?' asked Harry. I had never heard him so agitated, not even when he bought what he thought to be Hitler's suicide pistol on eBay.

'It's Claudia,' he said. 'She's on her way.'

I sank into a faux eighteenth-century easy chair. 'What? Here? When? Why?'

'Don't be surprised if she brings a chainsaw. She said you hadn't been returning her calls. And she sounded really mad.'

'Mad' I try to explain to my German friends can mean crazy or angry. Harry seemed to suggest she was both: mad^2.

'She came round to see me,' Harry continued. 'Says she wants some clarity between you and her. Lucky she didn't kill me actually.'

'And you just told her where I was? No attempt to mislead her?'

'You know my motto. Never knowingly lie to a woman, especially if she is on the warpath.'

To my certain knowledge this had never been one of Harry's mottos. I was silent for a while pondering the significance of the impending arrival of Claudia. Perhaps I could switch hotels and throw her off the track.

On the other end of the line, Harry was getting restless. 'Are you still there? Look at it this way, you could put them both through their paces. Then it really would be a road-test. You know: who performs the best in a crisis? Tick. Who has most passion? Tick.'

'Who murders most efficiently? Tick. Who castrates with most pain? Tick,' I added.

'Exactly! Now you're getting into the spirit of things. Anyway, so I followed Claudia to the station. It was great – I was like the Philip Marlowe of downtown Berlin! I'm certain she didn't spot me.'

'So she's due in three hours or so?'

The train to Rostock was slow at this time of the evening. And Claudia would have to get to Heiligendamm. I just had time to devise an avoidance strategy.

'Well, actually,' said Harry, sheepishly, 'I had a few drinks after seeing her get on the train. Met my mate Matthias… ' I dimly recalled a perpetually drunken colleague from *Der Spiegel*. 'And we caught up on old times. You know how it is. Anyway, I'm ringing you now.'

'You're trying to tell me, that she could be arriving… ?'

'Yes.' Harry's voice was deeply serious. 'Any minute now.'

Sure enough, as I stumbled back towards Renata, I heard the dining room doors open with a crash, a burst of sound so urgently invasive, so loaded with negative energy it could have been the act of a poltergeist. As I passed the diners I could see them looking up from their plates of handcrafted pasta to inspect the apparition. I, however, did not turn. The presence of Claudia was already obvious to me without empirical confirmation. The longer I could delay the moment that she spotted me, the longer I would live. There was a strong case for throwing myself on the floor and hiding under a tablecloth.

Renata, blissfully ignorant of the approaching storm, smiled at me as I took my seat.

'Crisis at the office?' she asked, with a gentleness to her voice. She had dried her tears.

'Life is a crisis,' I replied, hearing the click-click-click of urban cowboy boots coming across the dining room floor and knowing, with absolute certainty, that I had been spotted.

I looked down at my plate. Even the food seemed to want to hide under a curled leaf of salad.

Then the clicking stopped. Beside me there was the sound of heavy breathing. My gaze stayed fixed on the remains of the plate.

'So,' said Claudia, for it was she. 'This… is Renata!'

The two women stared at each other.

Claudia wore a denim jacket, tight Diesel jeans, and her red blouse – my favourite – was open by two buttons. She looked like a matador getting ready to drive her sword between the eyes of a defeated bull; the bull being me. Her whole body smelled of rage. If you could have bottled that smell and sold it as perfume you could have made a fortune selling it to the US Marines or to the customers in Berlin's sado-masochistic clubs. Renata had drawn herself up in her seat, straight backed and alert. Her fist was clenched round a fork.

'Yes,' she said calmly, 'and who might you be?' The words came out in a controlled staccato.

Claudia did not answer but pulled a chair from the neighbouring table and turned it back to front. She straddled it. The back of the chair was body armour. It was a man's pose.

'Oh, hello, Claudia,' I said. 'What a surprise! What a nice surprise. Renata, this is Claudia. She is, er… a friend from the gym.'

Claudia exploded.

'Is that what I am? Someone you go on the cross-trainer with? A changing-room buddy?'

Renata cleared her throat.

'Perhaps somebody could put me in the picture?'

Claudia turned to her. 'I think your "boyfriend" had better do that,' said Claudia, almost spitting out the words. 'A friend from the gym! What do you think we have been doing for the past four months?'

'Yes, what have you been doing for the past four months?' Renata's voice was rising. The tables nearby were showing interest. This was not the kind of performance one usually got on an all-inclusive mini-break.

My preferred strategy, in obedience to my male cowardice gene, would have been to let the women argue it out while I quietly withdrew. Then they would either settle their differences or a victor would emerge out of the Darwinian struggle. But it was already too late for that.

Claudia was certainly in fighting mood. A cartoonist would have described her with steam coming out of her ears and nose, and a black, thunderous cloud suspended over her head.

'Well,' I said to Renata fawningly, 'you mustn't think I have been having an affair…'

'Oh my God,' exclaimed Claudia, 'what a creep! Shall I list some of the things we have done over the past summer?'

'Claudia!' This, with some alarm. 'Stop it!'

'No, please, do tell,' said Renata. Two pink spots had appeared on her cheekbones. She looked me deep in the eyes. 'Are you trying to tell me that all the time, we have been together, you have been seeing this…' She pointed at Claudia without looking at her. 'This woman?'

'God, it's not like that.' And it really was not. 'I mean, Claudia and I, erm, we never made love or anything. It's just that two friendships developed in parallel.' I decided not to explain further.

The waiter arrived with dessert. Cowed by the force of our tabletop drama, he mumbled out his offering: 'A symphony of walnuts hand-shelled in communion with cappuccino ice cream composed from a special recipe prepared for the Duke of Mecklenburg.'

Renata waved him away.

'What do you mean, "never made love"?' screeched Claudia. 'Are we in love or not? What is the point of setting each other love tests if you are betraying me the whole time? You haven't even the courtesy to reply to my e-mails.'

Her voice grew gruffer. I recognised the change of tone. It was the moment when Claudia stopped being a political animal, pitching her speech cadences for applause, and let her real feelings show.

'I thought we had an understanding.'

'Love tests?' asked Renata, now clearly very, very angry. 'What the hell are love tests?'

'He ran the marathon for me,' said Claudia, and I understood then how proud she had been. For her, the marathon had been a sign of her complete control over me, the subordination of my will to hers. It was a combination of male self-assertion – man conquers own weak body – and emasculation. It was a perfect expression of post-feminist thinking. Love, I realised in a unpleasant flash, was for Claudia an extension of politics by other means.

Even so, the only way for me to regain control of the situation was to keep the women apart.

The dining room was almost entirely silent. Only the clanking of pots and pans from the kitchen broke the funeral calm. Even Ruediger had stopped boasting about his successes as a water-skier and had subtly altered the position of his chair to catch the twists and turns of our argument. The word 'marathon' must have activated him. It took a great deal to make a listener out of Ruediger.

'Look,' I said, 'you both know I've always respected the individual privacy of women.'

It sounded pompous but I was scrambling for delay. 'We should talk somewhere else. Claudia, why don't you go to the bar and wait for me there? Renata and I will finish dessert and we can talk rationally together.'

'Ha!' said Claudia, and stayed firmly rooted to her chair. 'You're not getting out of it as easily as that.'

I glanced at Renata, certain that she would agree to the scheme. She loved ice cream and it would have been sad for her to see it disappear into the kitchen.

But, no. Renata too was on the warpath.

'But you didn't run the marathon,' she blurted out.

'Of course I did. Ask Claudia.' Reluctantly, Claudia nodded.

'So what were those maps I found in Mac's food bag earlier?'

'What maps?' Claudia was starting to look at me very closely.

'Different marathon routes. With big yellow arrows showing short-cuts.'

'Renata, I don't know what you're talking about.' But I did. Harry had photocopied marathon maps and I had stupidly forgotten to shred them. More, I had absent-mindedly stuffed the paper together with the dog food.

'One of them had the number of an intern. Over his name it clearly said: YOUR RUNNER.'

Renata took out the crumpled sheet. She turned to Claudia.

'Maybe we should ring him, Claudia? What do you think?'

The women were now on the same side. It was a pincer movement, encirclement. The classic nightmare of every general.

'You rummaged round in my personal papers?' I noticed Ruediger in the middle distance, taking in every word. 'That was a bit cheap, wasn't it?'

'Not half as cheap as digging in a woman's handbag,' she said. Aha, so she *had* seen me.

Claudia was aghast at the revelations.

'You... you cheated at the marathon? To win me? How can you ever begin to explain that?'

'It's too public here,' I said, 'you're both making a spectacle out of yourselves.'

All I could think was please, please can we settle this out of Ruediger's gaze.

'This is not the United Nations,' said Claudia, her voice rising almost into a shout. 'We are not cutting secret deals. If you have something to say, say it now. To both of us.' But there was no time for my reply. The barrage had begun.

Renata: 'Although I'm beginning to think you have nothing to say.'

Claudia: 'And that you just want to play her off against me. And vice versa.'

Renata: 'And that you are an utter cynic!'

Claudia: 'Calculating!'

Renata: 'Deceitful!'

Claudia: 'Manipulative!'

Abruptly, Claudia stood up and, with the muscular force of someone who lifted weights three times a week, slapped me. It hurt.

Renata too got up from her seat. She grabbed the champagne out of the ice bucket, shook it up and shot the gassy foam at my face.

'You deserve a lot worse than that!' hissed Claudia, and seemed ready to garrotte me.

'You don't understand,' I bleated.

'Wrong. We understand perfectly,' said Renata.

'Come, come, ladies. It's time everyone calmed down a bit.' This, from Ruediger, who had decided to play peace-broker. He spread his arms out wide, determined that the dining room should notice the grandness of his gesture. 'Why don't I take you lovely ladies to the bar and buy you a gin and tonic.' He flashed his white teeth at me. 'Very English drink, G and T. The English are so very good at diplomacy, don't you think?'

'Stay out of this, Ruediger,' I growled.

'No,' said Renata standing up so quickly she almost knocked over her chair. 'He's right. I don't want to sit next to you for another minute.' She looked very attractive. Her scarf had come loose and I glimpsed her smooth pale neck. I would have liked to kiss it but this was definitely not the moment.

'But Renata, what about your ice cream?' That was my last, weak trump card. Too late. The two women were clicking their way out of the dining room accompanied by a smug-looking Ruediger.

An English gentleman's self-esteem is built up by his expensive, traditional education which is comprised of years of bullying, flogging, home-sickness, emotional neglect and brutal athleticism. If he survives school, an Englishman feels that he is invincible. Nothing, almost nothing, can dent his complacency, his sense that he is one of the masters of the universe.

But take two women, two German women, and let them loose on an unsuspecting English victim and, well, nothing much remains. I stayed in the restaurant alone. After half an hour of character assassination – coffee and cognac turned away, the waiter close to nervous collapse – I felt like a zookeeper mauled at feeding time by two misguided lions.

Perhaps, just perhaps, they were a little bit right. Perhaps there was something morally dubious about maintaining parallel relationships. But, after all, Moslems were allowed four wives, provided each were treated equally. And European society was ruled by people who had serial marriages.

The truly immoral, or amoral (the English always found it difficult to make a distinction) element was that I was seeking marriage to escape a cripplingly-high tax debt.

Even that goal was being pursued out of the best motives: to find enough money to support my father in his dotage.

Yet the women knew nothing of my tax problems. They were furious only because they existed in duplicate. Could this, I wondered, as they had battered me earlier with their low thoughts on my low character, could this be a German phenomenon, an offshoot of the women's movement? Could it be that knowing, liking and kissing two women was as heinous a crime as polygamy?

Germans, I knew, had an obsession with – and a fear of – choice. The decision to provide households with black, brown, green and blue rubbish bins was discussed for the best part of a decade. In the sixteenth century, Germans would spend hours debating the postulates of Martin Luther. In the twenty-first century, they talked about rubbish, the price of recycling, whether to wash yoghurt containers, whether condoms belonged in a yellow or a green bin. Making choices was uniquely difficult for Germans, so when a man – and an Englishman to boot – was unable to choose between two German women, a moral debate was conjured up.

It seemed unfair. I hated causing hurt. Avoiding choice was a way of avoiding pain. Why couldn't they understand that? Had there been an ethical breakdown – or a linguistic collapse?

Renata and Claudia had left the dining room more enraged by my passivity than by arguments. We had provided a unique spectacle to those guests on their day-of-German-unity outing, comparable to the days when women used to wrestle in mud on the Reeperbahn.

One man raised his wine glass to me; Rose, now alone at her table, threw me a shy smile. On another table money changed hands. Clearly, they had been betting on the outcome of the three-sided boxing match.

It was a reasonable question: who had won the argument? Who had lost? For me, the answer was simple. I was on a losing streak. Life could not get much grimmer.

The room had fallen quiet again after the departure of the women, my women. I did not want to think about what they were now plotting against me. The bill arrived, together with three mint chocolates, which I stuffed into my pocket for my poor, innocent dog languishing in the bedroom. The waiter had made the transition from obsequious to surly without passing through the intermediate phase of charming. I handed him a credit card, as worn down and as tired as its owner. The waiter could barely conceal his glee when he returned.

'I'm sorry, Sir. Your card has not been accepted.'

'What am I supposed to do,' I said taking out my exasperation on the smug, pigeon-chested waiter. 'Do the bloody washing-up?'

'No, Sir,' came the terse reply, 'we have a very good Bosch machine for this purpose.'

I waited for him to recite all the wash programmes but he stayed awkwardly silent. Then, a brainwave.

'Send the bill to the lady at Herr Matussek's table,' I said. He plodded off dutifully.

Rose, I could see, understood immediately and with a quick flick of the pen, faked Ruediger's signature on my bill. She grinned at me. The waiter smiled too (she had obviously given a generous tip).

My phone rang. I picked it up with trepidation. Which of the two women could it be?

'Hello, son,' said a familiar voice, 'I've got some news.'

'Not now, Dad,' I said sadly and switched off the mobile.

Chapter Thirteen

Five Scenes from a Wedding

Scene 1

'Are you ready?'

Dad was impatient. His hands wandered, looking for a firm perch. First he pulled at the sleeves of his morning coat, then at his shirt cuffs. A hand on his tie, a tug on his waistcoat. He even licked the tip of his finger and stroked his eyebrow.

'Good God, you look a mess,' he said, after finishing his preening, and turning his gaze to my outfit.

Dad was right. It was no way to dress for a wedding. Useless to explain to him the many hurdles that Germany puts in the way of a man trying to dress up on a threadbare budget.

'It's all right for you, you've had the same morning suit since you married Mum.'

'God rest her soul. Last wore it to your cousin Anne-Marie's wedding back in 1979. Been in mothballs ever since.'

'You or the suit?'

'Less of your lip, son,' he said, making as if to clip me behind the ears. I ducked, pretending it was a serious threat, cricking my back in the process.

It really had been difficult to find the appropriate clothing. Germans dressed down, turning up in lounge suits at parties which were clearly marked 'evening dress', and wearing jeans to the opera. Berlin was worst of all. About the only time you saw a suit with tails was at the Philharmonic when the frontline violinists flicked back their jackets in a single-reflex movement to prevent them being creased. Later at the stage door, you could see the violinists leaving in dishevelled jeans, their smart togs tucked into black garment bags as if they were a cause for shame.

In the end I had to go to an Oxfam charity shop and dig out a grey, coffee-stained morning coat and a top hat that had last been used by a children's magician. All for forty euros. It was about as far as my budget stretched. But – and here Dad had a point – even intensive dry cleaning had failed to transform the outfit into a suit worthy of the big day. It smelled, faintly, of dead people.

'I suppose it does lack a certain flair,' I admitted to my father. 'The real thing costs money.'

'Don't talk to me about money,' said Dad, in the firm, gruff voice I had not heard since childhood. I had noticed a barely perceptible change in him. He had started to carry himself better. Like a man who was again in charge of his life. His dandruff had gone.

Two months had passed since the catastrophe on the Baltic. The days had become shorter, colder and wetter; too cold even for the hardiest FKK faithful. It was the time of year when Germans moved from outdoors to indoors. The streets of Berlin, as darkness started to gather – sometimes as early as just after lunch – were depopulated. People moved into the wind, head down, collars up, diving into shops not because they could afford to buy anything but because of the artificial light and the briefly borrowed warmth.

After the catastrophe, my first instinct was to flee Berlin, to stop brooding about how I had let everybody down (Renata, Claudia, my father, my neglected friends). If the money had been there, I would have sought refuge in Greece, an uncomplicated place where I could walk with the dog on the beach and catch some sunshine. Instead, I had plunged into work.

Harry had, through his nefarious contacts, discovered a man who had a collection of Hitler's toothbrushes. Deep in eastern Germany we visited the collection, stored like fine wine in a specially-cooled cellar.

'You are standing in front of the biggest deposit of Führer DNA in the world,' said the collector, a forty-five-year-old schoolteacher who had retired early to pursue his perverse hobby.

He had insisted that we wear Michael Jackson-style face masks, hair covers and latex gloves. Each of the twelve brushes came with a certificate showing its history. Two had been used in Hitler's Wolf's Lair bunker, and one in the Obersalzberg, his Alpine bolthole.

'Even if they are all genuine,' I asked the former teacher, 'what would be the point of having Hitler's DNA?'

The man looked at me as if I were mad. So did Harry.

'For God's sake, man. Get a grip,' said Harry. 'If you've got Hitler's genetic material you might one day be able to clone him.'

It was at that moment that I lost faith in my profession. While Harry continued to interview the guardian of Hitler's dental hygiene, I went outside and took a few deep breaths under an apple tree. The obsession with the Third Reich was no longer healthy; it had become a kind of compulsive voyeurism. The toothbrush-man was obviously mad; so, less obviously, were we.

'Are you all right?' asked Harry. I grunted. 'I think you might be in the wrong job.'

Not only that, I was in the wrong place at the wrong time.

I had tried to write an apology note to Renata but it had ended up as a sad appeal for understanding and as a treatise on the need for dishonesty in love.

It was a bit like the letters written – on the orders of probation officers – from prisoners to their victims. Something along the lines of: 'I'm really, really sorry I stole your handbag but I needed the money because I have three starving children at home because their selfish mother left them with me, saying I was an alcoholic which is not true, not really, really true, and anyway if you had the kind of upbringing I've had, on the streets of Glasgow, broken glass shoved in your face when you're seven, well, then you would have a drink or two and probably steal a handbag stupidly left unguarded in the bus.'

I had seen that kind of letter during university law classes and laughed at the primitive self-pity. Now I was attempting a similar correspondence with Renata. It did not work. I crumpled up the paper and let the relationship slump into silence. Claudia too had pulled up the drawbridge, not replying to the messages I left on her answering machine.

In the end, I gave up. The truth was that I had misled and humiliated two women, and my motives had been wrong. This had come as a kind of biblical revelation to me. Man was made for the pursuit of love. Everything else – the invention of the wheel, hunting deer, drawing on the walls of caves – was subordinate to this drive. But civilisation had taught us that love is bound by rules. The basic rule is that the purpose of a loving partnership is the fulfilment of both partners, not the tax man.

By those standards I had failed both my German women. They had not wanted much from me. Only a kind of integrity.

All this had gone through my head in the corridor the night of the catastrophe. After cutting Dad off, I had felt guilty.

The whole escapade, after all, was an attempt to restore my relationship with him. So I had taken Mac out to the beach and, with the seagulls wheeling overhead like Apaches round a wagon train, I rang my father back. His news had been shattering and changed everything.

Scene 2

Downstairs, Harry sounded his horn. I popped my head out of the window.

'Come on,' he shouted, 'we're running late. We've got to get the cake.' I ran down the stairs, the only exercise I had had all day.

'You nervous? You certainly look it.'

'Me, no, of course not.' I could barely control my shaking leg.

'Well, I am,' said Harry.

The cake shop was a dusty-looking place hidden, like a brothel, behind a busy tree in a side street behind the Ku'damm. I had suggested the more traditional option – the Vienna Konditorei. It was the only establishment in Berlin to apply the Austrian love of sugar, pastry and exhibitionism to its work (for Austrians every cake was a wedding cake – an extravagant operatic performance). The decision, however, had gone against me. The cake, the centrepiece of any good marriage (the more marzipan you eat on wedding day, the longer you will stay together), was to come from one of the last bastions of the old West Berlin: a place with plush green seats suitable for widows with haemorrhoids, and forty watt lighting.

A conventional wedding cake rises in layers like a pile of hat boxes plastered with icing sugar. On top there is almost always a little man holding hands with a woman in a wedding dress. The overall effect is usually kitsch but then, as Tony told me in our last heart-to-heart session, weddings are kitsch. And since this was a Christmas wedding, we had to brace ourselves for a veritable orgy of kitsch.

Yet the cake that was brought out by the sallow-faced baker's assistant was not like that at all.

It had a long, slender body with a slight bulge at the end. Two flat pieces of hardened icing sugar jutted out on either side. The whole cake had been sprayed with green food colouring.

'Pistachio green,' said the baker.

'RAF green,' said Harry. He was right. The cake was a crude reconstruction of a Lancaster bomber. The solid-sugar protuberances were wings, and the tailfin looked as if it had been made with chocolate covered wafers. The confectioner painted the smiling faces of a man and a woman in the cockpit. The artfully written inscription read, HAPPY LANDINGS. I just hoped it did not taste as bad as it looked.

'It was what the bride wanted,' said the baker.

'The bride?' I couldn't quite believe that.

'Yes, a man came in with a diagram and said the lady insisted exactly on this design. It was very difficult. We have never made a bomber before.'

I did not like the sound of this but Harry was anxious to move on. We had a list of jobs to be accomplished before the wedding service: collecting the bay trees that would line the path to the reception, a visit to the florist, countless phone calls.

'We'll take it,' snapped Harry. 'On this day the bride is always right.'

And so we hoisted the cake onto the front seat of the car.

'Shall we strap it with a seat belt?' I asked Harry.

'Nah, the airbag will catch it,' he said.

We zig-zagged through Berlin. The sponsored Christmas lights garlanded the shopping boulevards and even though it was still morning they helped clear the gloom. Loudspeakers played 'Last Christmas' sung by George Michael at a time when everybody thought he still liked girls. Six portly men dressed as Father Christmas marched down the shopping boulevard, each assigned to a different department store.

'Don't worry,' said Harry, looking at me in the rear-view mirror. 'It will all go smoothly. Everyone gets nervous before a wedding. Especially before weddings like this.'

'Thanks,' I said, though it was hardly a cause for cheer.

'At least your dad is happy.'

'Is he?' I couldn't quite believe it.

'And, let's face it, so are you. Now look on the back seat. Do you see a book with flowers on it?'

I rummaged among the wedding debris: a pile of invitations that someone had forgotten to post, lists of priests, hotel brochures. Slowly it dawned on me how much work Harry had put into the organisation of the wedding. It had been a logistical nightmare. The requested bay trees were a ridiculous expense that could only be to the benefit of one guest, Dr von Landauer, who was bringing a 'surprise guest' (a labrador or old English sheepdog, most likely). The canine guest would surely be grateful for a tree or two.

'Now,' said Harry, 'tell me what the flowers mean.'

There had been a mix-up with the flower arrangements. The florist had lost the list and no one could remember what had been ordered.

'Edelweiss,' I read. 'Your beauty is overwhelming.'

'Forget it,' said Harry. 'Too expensive'.

'Lily,' I continued. 'Unattainable beauty.'

'Too smelly,' said Harry, steering with one hand, while stabilising the cake with the other.

'How about amaryllis?' I said, 'It means "bitter pride". You can get them in red.'

'Well, that's about right. And they're a bargain. They grow in fields, don't they? We could virtually pick them ourselves.'

'Not before Christmas, I'm afraid.'

We had a pleasantly irrelevant conversation about horticulture. It took my mind off the ceremonies ahead; the guests, the stares, the sense that a truly bizarre marriage was about to be sealed.

And then the phone rang.

'I've got some bad news, son.' Dad's voice was trembling.

'Tell me.' A terrible sense of foreboding swept over me.

'I've lost the ring.'

'Oh, for God's sake, Dad. I told you to give it to someone else for safe keeping.' I should never have trusted him with it.

'It just slipped into the toilet.'

'Did you flush?'

'Of course, I did. What do you take me for? I always flush! Not like you.'

'Can you just concentrate on the problem rather than just flailing round?' It was one of the most unpleasant characteristics of my father in crisis: the panicked search for a scapegoat.

'Just don't fish. I'll get back to you.'

We rang Tony from the car. Long years of Anglo-German fatherhood had made him an excellent plumber. So far his children had thrown an IUD coil, two Swiss Army knives, a gold cigarette lighter and a cufflink into their toilet. All successfully retrieved.

'It's a suction problem,' he said. 'I'll go have a look.'

I sensed he was almost relieved to be out of his house.

'Good,' I said. Harry looked out of the car window.

Would it be good? Was everything going to turn out OK after all?

Scene 3

The role of an usher at a wedding is not very demanding. You stand in the porch of a church and watch people arrive, cursing the snow and the traffic. Women change from their winter boots into more graceful shoes and you offer them your arm so that they don't overbalance.

You show them to their places. The German guests, friends and relatives of the bride, were supposed to be directed to the pews on the right side of the church. The English guests were shown to the left side. The correct formula is to ask the guest, 'Bride or groom?', a laconic way of asking which team they're on.

Tom, naturally, took matters too far.

'Are you with us, or the krauts? Oh, you're one of us. Very good. The green coat fooled me. Well, here's the order of service. Take a seat on the left and try to stay awake! Hah, hah.'

I did not recognise most of the guests, though there was no mistaking the grimace on their faces when Tom put on his little racist act. Even the veteran RAF men – some of whom I recognised from the reunion – were obviously unhappy with Tom's joshing talk of 'jerries' and 'krauts'.

'Who is that nasty little man?' asked the red-faced paratrooper who had known my father. His breath was already heavy with whiskey.

'That's Tom. Lancaster crew with my dad. He's going to be best man.'

'Good God,' said the paratrooper, 'I hope he doesn't mess it up. Your mother would have turned in her grave.'

'Well, I don't think Mum had much of a say in this wedding.'

It was with some relief that I recognised familiar faces. Becky had come, looking radiant and girlish in a lacy dress, accompanied by her motorbike-jacket wearing girlfriend. Their motorbike (complete with sidecar) was parked outside.

'I am so proud that your father is tying the knot,' said Becky. She had always got on well with my dad and even seemed to enjoy listening to his endless stories.

'Good that you're here,' I said. 'That you're both here.' I could not remember the name of Becky's butch lover. 'And who is this young man?' Between them was a seven-year-old Asian boy, neatly dressed in a suit, his slick, black hair combed back.

'This is Kim,' said Becky. 'We've adopted him. It was time, you know, to expand our family.'

The two women passed into the church with their son, leaving me wondering whether things would have turned out differently if I had had a child with Becky.

The guests filed in, perhaps a hundred or more. Some of them, complete strangers, shook my hand vigorously as if it was me, and not Dad, who was getting married. After months of moaning about the inverted childhood of Dad, about how I had to look after my increasingly babyish dad, I was now being treated as a proud parent.

'You must be so happy,' crowed one fat matron who didn't seem to fit into the guest category of either the bride or the groom.

'Yes, yes,' I said, 'very proud.'

Then I spotted a familiar, heart-stopping face. Renata.

'Hello,' she said shyly.

'Hello,' I said.

'I'm not really invited but Chris knows the priest and so we thought it would be all right to come along.'

It was strange to see Renata. I had imagined that I would bump into her in a cafe in a year or two, when my sense of guilt had ebbed and I had regained my balance. It seemed somehow too soon to see her now. My pulse was racing.

'This is Chris.'

A mountainous man blocked out the thin light in the porch. He was bearded and seemed to be bursting out of his jacket. Most of the bulk was evidently muscle. He was, I thought, a Canadian lumberjack and I decided, then and there, I would not get into an argument with him.

'Chris is a bass guitarist,' continued Renata, 'and he plays in a Christian heavy-metal band with the priest.'

'Of course,' I said, noticing out of the corner of my eye that Tom was getting into an argument.

'Chris,' said Renata to the lumberjack, 'give me a second, OK?'

We shuffled into an alcove full of brushes and mops. I felt a great wave of tenderness for Renata. I hoped she was all right.

'Are you all right?'

'I wanted to ask you the same question.' She smiled.

'I feel such a shit.'

'You hurt me.'

'I tried to write to you.'

'I guessed.'

'It was a kind of madness. I wanted to solve all my problems all at once.'

'I don't think I could ever be one of your solutions. I'm a complicated woman.'

'I know that. I'm sorry.'

We were silent for a while.

'I'd better get back,' I said, 'before Tom starts World War Three.'

Renata nodded. 'Friends?'

'Yes,' I said, relief seeping through my bones, 'Friends.'

As we returned to the porch, I said, 'That Chris seems a nice guy.'

'One of the best,' she said, with utter conviction. And blushed.

'I wouldn't want to meet him in a dark alleyway though. He looks like he could crush me in his left hand.'

Renata punched me playfully.

Harry, fortunately, had appeared on the doorstep of the church to separate Tom from the German guests he had been harassing.

'Tom,' he said firmly, 'you are best man. Your place is on or near the altar. Go there. Please.'

Then Harry bent down slightly so that he could whisper directly into the war vet's ear. 'Or I will sock you one. I have no respect for age or war medals. Scram!'

Drained of colour, Tom obeyed orders, limping up the aisle.

'Right,' said Harry, as he saw me approach. 'That's settled.' He looked at me closely.

'You seem different. Something happen?'

'I've just started to relax for the first time this year.'

'Ah,' he said, 'the wonders of transcendental meditation.'

'Something like that.'

'Well, why don't you leave the ushering to me and check that the organist has got the right sheet music up there. I didn't much like the look of him.'

Grateful that Harry had everything in hand, and with one word bouncing round my skull ('friends?'), I climbed the stairs to the organ in the gallery. It provided a magnificent viewing point. Spread out in front of me was a sea of hats that seemed to bob like buoys on the tide. It was a sea split down the middle as if by Moses.

On the left there were pink, squashy hats, some with veils and appliqué with pearls. Those were the Englishwomen who always, in socially insecure situations, go for pink, the colour of British flesh.

On the right, heads were covered with more elegant, black, feathery creations. A bit funereal perhaps but at least they did not look like supermarket puddings. Those were the German women.

As for the men, they looked just about the same as the women from my point of view, high up with the organist. The Englishmen looked, as usual, more neglected, their hair curling up over their collars. My stained morning coat was just about within the British norm. The Germans, by contrast, sat up straight, did not hack up nicotine phlegm and did not slip out for one last visit to the lavatory.

The most unconventional presence among the contingent on the right was Ingo von Landauer. I was not sure how he had landed on the guest list and I was even less certain how he had won the priest's permission to bring not one, but two *huntin'*, *shootin'*, *fishin'* dogs into the church. The slobbery hounds panted like turbines. Still, it was a Protestant church – the kind where priests complain about George Bush – and more or less anything was allowed. Certainly, the organist did not seem to be bothered by the dogs. He was that special brand of churchman: an earring in his left ear, highlights in his hair, Pepe jeans.

'Don't be nervous,' he said, no doubt observing the way I was fiddling with my watch. 'Brides are always late. It's what brides do.'

'Not this one,' I said. 'Have you ever been married?'

'I'm not really the marrying kind,' he lisped. I thought I saw a flash in his mouth. He had a pierced tongue.

'I think I'd better join my dad.' I could see him pacing up and down with the special aura of irritation that I remembered from childhood. He was capable, without uttering a word, of signalling an immense discomfort with the world around him. Now he was sending off a woman in 1950s horn-rimmed glasses to rearrange the amaryllis that I had bought with Harry. I spotted him whispering to Tom, who demonstratively patted his pocket.

'Everything all right, Dad?' I asked, after descending the iron staircase from the organist's nest.

'Of course it's not. I don't understand how you can be so calm. Look at the guests, they're completely restless.'

'At least we got the ring back.'

'That Tony fellow must have elastic arms. He went right round the hidden bend and pulled it out.'

I crinkled my nose at the thought.

'Well, I hope you washed it afterwards.'

'Aye, and gave it to Tom for safe keeping.'

Somehow this thought did not provide the necessary reassurance.

The church of St Ethelred the Unready had been a strange choice for the wedding. It had been built in the 1920s with the help of a donation from a German steel baron (perhaps he sensed that his conscience would soon be troubling him). In any case, the aesthetics of the building was close to that of an iron foundry – bare red-brick walls, angular and unadorned. I preferred a bit of show-biz glitz in my religion (maybe I was a closet Catholic, more comfortable with incense and rosaries). The one beautiful part of the church was the stained-glass window. Originally it had shown St Ethelred surrounded by men in stormtrooper uniforms, painted at a time when it was still possible to be a Nazi and a Christian. But the Allied bombing raids of late 1944 shattered the glass. When the windows were rebuilt in the 1950s – with the generous help of the former steel magnate who had switched to making bubble cars – they showed a suffering Christ surrounded by weeping women. The glass was deep blood-red, gold and Prussian blue. As the winter sunlight shone through the windows, the altar became a patchwork of strong colours. The guests stopped shifting from one buttock to another and gazed at the play of light.

My eyes were fixed, though, on the open main door of the church. Harry, dressed in a neat, crisp suit and smoothly shaven, had telegraphed the agreed signal. The bridal car was on its way. I waved to the organist in the gallery to prepare him for action and walked swiftly to the side where Dad and the woman in glasses were moving flower vases.

'No time for that,' I said in a loud whisper, 'she's almost here. Better get into position.'

'You don't understand,' puffed Dad, straining under the weight of a stone container that he was moving well away from the altar. 'Brigitte here' – he nodded towards the woman in apricot – 'says the bride is allergic to amaryllis.'

'How would she know that?'

'Brigitte is bridesmaid of honour.'

'Oh,' I said. Nobody had told me that there were going to be bridesmaids. But then, I hadn't actually asked. I had just assumed this was going to be a mature wedding without the usual circus. After all, a woman who had ordered a wedding cake designed like a Lancaster could not fairly be described as a traditionalist. Still, it would explain why three unhappy looking women were sausaged into exceptionally ugly dresses in the front row.

The organist started suddenly to pump air into his pipes.

'Forget that now!' Dad dropped the vase with a loud echoing clang and scrambled into position as if his plane had been given the order to take-off.

Brigitte and the other apricots ran towards the door.

There, in a moment of theatre that seemed quite alien to this trim, no-nonsense woman, stood Mechthild Beckenbender. Her dress, more vanilla than white, seemed to tumble down her body onto the floor as if she had taken a shower in silk.

'Parachute silk,' said Tom, who was suddenly standing next to me. He smelled strangely and I could only hope that the ring had been as thoroughly cleaned as my father had promised.

'Don't be ridiculous,' I said, 'that was then, not now. Nobody makes wedding dresses out of parachutes any more.'

Tom fell into a grumpy silence, for which I was very grateful.

Hooked on Frau Beckenbender's arm was an unfamiliar figure: a double chinned man, several centimetres shorter than Frau Beckenbender, with a monocle. He looked like bank managers used to look before they started reading *Men's Health* and waxing their chests. Prosperous.

'It's Count von Budnitz,' muttered Harry. All the English members of the welcoming delegation had clustered together on the porch. 'Old family friend apparently. Has a stud farm in the Swabian alps. Fabulously rich.'

We all perked up at this last news item.

The pierced organist had struck up the bridal march, and the pair walked with exaggerated calm towards my father at the altar. Dad was looking very lonely. Tom moved forwards, patting his ring pocket. Harry and I slipped into pews near Landauer and his slobbery dogs.

'You're on the German side of the church,' he hissed.

'Don't be so bloody prejudiced, Ingo,' I snapped back. 'We're all European now. What are you doing here anyway?'

'I've been Frau Beckenbender's financial adviser for years!'

'Really?' I said, not sure what to make of the information.

It was only when Dad reached out his hand to Frau Beckenbender as she stepped up to the altar, only when I saw the look in his eyes as he pecked her cheek, that I fully realised the significance of the changes in the last months. In Dad's Heiligendamm phone call, his declaration of love for Frau Beckenbender had flabbergasted me. It was inconceivable to me that two, well, *old* people could talk in the vocabulary of adolescence. Old people were supposed to be into companionship not passion.

'It just clicked,' Dad had said. And then hearing my long silence. 'I was hoping you would be happy for us.'

Well, I wasn't really. I do not like to be ambushed by events. My father, it seemed, had tipped over the edge into lunacy, narrowly dodging senile dementia but plunging instead into teenage angst. Does she love me? Do I love her enough?

'Dad, shouldn't you be entering a period of prolonged reflection about the meaning of life, about what went wrong, about what you achieved and what you're proud of?'

'My God,' retorted Dad, 'I fathered an accountant.' And put the phone down.

In the end it was Frau Beckenbender who convinced me that their liaison was serious, rather than the result of mixing the wrong kind of medication.

After our dinner in Prenzlauer Berg, Frau Beckenbender had decided to resume contact with my father. They had started to write to each other. Not e-mails, of course, but a good old-fashioned epistolary romance. What had started as an act of sympathy, had flowered into something far more. 'He and his terrible Tom came to visit me in my cottage in the country,' Frau Beckenbender told me.

I didn't even know she had an out-of-town place.

'Something sparked between us. We sent Tom into the wine cellar and didn't see him again for three hours. So we talked and talked. Bob – your dad – and I. He told me how horribly scared he had been in the air, how he had even thought about deserting. Desertion! Can you imagine that?'

I could not.

'Your father is so brave, so unconventionally brave. He doesn't run away from complicated problems.'

Could this have been a criticism of me? I studied Frau Beckenbender, suddenly so alive, glowing with the discovery of a late love as we talked on my Berlin sofa, and realised that no, she was not wielding a stiletto, there were no reproaches.

'I told him about what it was like to be a refugee in your own land, to have to abandon everything, knowing that you had become worthless. It was irrelevant to anybody whether you were alive or dead.'

I nodded slowly. Frau Beckenbender had always been reluctant to talk about those years. Instead we had used the exchange of recipes as a kind of meta-language.

'And then he started to cry.'

'What? Dad?' It was difficult to imagine.

'And then I started to cry.'

'And one thing led to another?'

'We opened our hearts, it released us. So, of course, we realised that this was more than a moment. When two people belong together, they have to take the next logical step. How do you say in English? They have to be determined.'

I thought about this for a while, sipping peppermint tea that had turned cold. But all I could think of asking was, 'What happened to Tom?'

'He drank three bottles of my late burgundy. He was too heavy to carry up the stairs, so we left him down there, covered him with a blanket. I think a man like Tom doesn't realise where he is or what he is doing for most of the time. He drank another bottle for breakfast, to wash out his mouth, so he said.'

'It would take a lot more than a late burgundy to clean up Tom's language,' I said.

I saw that if Dad and Frau Beckenbender got together, she would step up the pressure on my father to drop Tom. This seemed to be a very powerful reason to give my blessing to the wedding.

'Well, that's settled then,' I said, slapping my knees. 'I just wanted to make sure you weren't after my dad's money.'

Frau Beckenbender blenched.

'Whatever makes you think I would do that?' She seemed almost angry.

'Just a joke, Frau Beckenbender.'

Humour, I could see, might become a problem between them. On the other hand, I couldn't remember the last time that my father had cracked a joke worth laughing at. Perhaps life seemed less absurd or comic after the age of seventy.

Scene 4

The marriage ceremony was rolling along at the pace of Formula One. The priest – unshaven and with an earring that matched the one worn by the organist – may have been afraid that my father would not survive the ceremony. Certainly Dad's nose had turned the colour of a tomato, always a sign that he was under extreme stress.

Frau Beckenbender, Mechthild as I was going to have to call her, was a model of self-control. Her long train had been spread out by the three apricot bridesmaid sausages. The women were, I was assured by von Landauer, the unmarriageable daughters of underemployed aristocrats. Brigitte had a job in the Foreign Ministry, the last refuge of Germany's redundant nobles. One of the other girls helped out with charity auctions, and improved her income by selling gossip to *Bunte*. The other, beefier, bridesmaid sold hunting guns and Barbour jackets in the hunting shop, Franconia Jagd. Compared to these virginal assistants, Frau Beckenbender looked, despite her advanced age, radiantly attractive, agile and clever. Dad, I reflected, had done well.

'Do you take this man, Robert, as your lawfully wedded husband and promise to take care of him?'

I glanced over at Harry, who looked paler than any of us, and wondered whether all was well with him. He was an alpha wolf, a quintessential loner. Throughout our friendship he had helped organise my life, yet he had rarely shown his own feelings. That, of course, was an English weakness. When I had asked him to organise Dad's wedding, he had jumped into action, digging out addresses of long-lost pilots, working out the order of service and persuading unemployed Kurdish taxi drivers to run a shuttle service between the church and the Allied Museum where the reception was to be held.

Why did he do it? Why did he plough so much energy into my life?

'I'm a broken-family fixer,' he told me. 'That's what I'm good at – helping people sort themselves out.'

'But I don't have a broken family,' I protested.

'Who are you kidding? You would have lost your dad one way or another if you had let things drift.'

He was right. I felt a surge of warmth for him.

From the altar came a booming, 'I do!'

It was the newly confident voice of my about-to-be-married father.

As Frau Beckenbender recited the vows I reflected that they went beyond cliché, that they retained a powerful simplicity, which captured the essence of a good life.

'I, Mechthild Sophie Hildegard take you Robert Hubert to be my husband, to have and to hold from this day forward, for better, for worse… '

Over on the English half of the church I caught the gaze of Becky. She smiled. The vows hadn't held for us, but she had found herself, and had never lost faith in marriage or family. Her adopted child was picking his nose, smelling the snot, licking it, rolling it into a ball and then flicking the missile across the pews. No doubt I would have done the same at his age.

'…for richer, for poorer… '

Ingo sniggered as if this line was a huge joke. I was still crippled by worry about my finances. True, I no longer had to fret too much about supporting my father – Frau Beckenbender seemed to have enough to keep the bailiffs from the door. That was a relief but my finances were still in a mess. The more I worked, the more

I was taxed. Surely, this was not a unique dilemma, but one that seemed to be plunging me further and further into debt.

' …in sickness and in health, to love and to cherish.'

I heard a cough behind me and turned round.

It was Renata, her smile more beatific than the saints on the painted glass. She did not notice me but let her head slip onto the shoulder of her bass guitarist. It was a gentle gesture. I understood that Renata, as fragile as eggshell, had found what she had been looking for – a protector. I was happy for her, and sad too that I had not been able to understand her needs.

'From this day forward, until death do us part.'

Suddenly Frau Beckenbender started to cough wildly and gasp for breath. Her face was simultaneously red, white and blue, like the face of a French football fan. Ingo and I leapt forward from the German pews, Harry from the English and von Landauer's dogs started to howl.

'Water, quick!' shouted my father, as his almost-bride slipped to the ground.

'Is there a doctor in the church?' called out the priest.

There wasn't. But Brigitte, the bespectacled maid of honour, knew exactly what was wrong. Reaching inside the cleavage of her apricot dress, she removed a small pillbox.

'Antihistamine tablets,' she said. 'Mechthild has an amaryllis allergy.' She glared at Harry and me, the flower purchasers. 'I warned you that this would happen.'

But nothing bad happened. Not really. Within minutes, Frau Beckenbender had been pronounced a Mrs and, though both partners were a bit wobbly on their feet, they clambered into the rented white Bentley for the drive to the reception. Someone had tastefully drawn the RAF circles on the back of the vehicle.

'Great British car,' said Tom.

'German actually,' said Harry.

Harry and I had agreed that we should try to contain the destructive potential of Tom as far as possible. During the wedding ceremony he had fulfilled his role as best man with unusual dignity. He only dropped the ring once and confused the congregation by smelling it and then rubbing it hard against his trousers. There was, however, trouble brewing. Tom had made clear that he was opposed to my father marrying Mechthild; indeed he was against the whole principle of the English marrying Germans.

'The rot set in when the Angles and Saxons got together,' he said, 'that's when England started to go downhill.'

I briefly tried to persuade him that the British Royal Family was in fact eighty-seven per cent German but to no avail. Tom's distaste for Germans was pathological and was resistant to rational argument. Dad couldn't grasp that Tom was not in fact his best friend but his best enemy. He could think of no better person to be best man than his former RAF crew mate.

'We'll have to be on our guard,' said Harry. 'It's too late to have him declared clinically insane.'

'Or arrested for racial incitement,' I chipped in.

At least Frau Beckenbender would not be shocked by Tom's antics. She had seen his true face during his drunken trip to her cottage.

Scene 5

Squadrons of empty cars already stood outside the museum when Harry and I finally arrived. I had asked Ruediger to persuade his bank to sponsor the reception to cut costs. Ruediger had agreed on one condition: that he was allowed to wear a kilt in a specially-designed Matussek tartan.

'Has he got anything underneath?' I asked Rose, who was standing by the door, nodding at guests without enthusiasm.

'There *is* nothing underneath,' she said. 'Believe me.'

I did, I did.

Even so, the surge of cash from the bank had lifted the quality of the reception beyond anything I could normally have afforded. The main hall resembled an aircraft hangar and an almost life-sized model of a plane, used in the Berlin Airlift, was suspended from the ceiling. Harry and I looked at each other wordlessly. If it came crashing down among the guests, it would be a wedding to remember. There was no time, however, for morbid thoughts. The guests were already being sorted into two long tables decked out in white linen. At the head table there was space for the bridal couple, Tom and Count von Budnitz. Above our heads was a huge banner announcing in mangled English, 'Deutsche Bank wishes to congratulate Mechthild and Robert. Long may they live!'

'Do you like the banner?' asked Ruediger eagerly.

'Great,' I said flatly. 'Thanks, Ruediger. Perhaps they should have got married in Deutsche Bank T-shirts.'

'Next time we'll get Telekom to do the job,' said Harry, creeping on us from behind. 'I like the pink helmets they wear in the Tour de France.'

In front of us there was a round table where the wedding cake was supposed to be positioned.

'Where's the cake?'

'Still in the kitchen,' said Harry. 'I've got a bad feeling about it. Do you think Frau Beckenbender would really have asked for a cake shaped like a Lancaster bomber? It doesn't seem like her at all.'

'What are you getting at?'

'I saw Tom lingering round the kitchen just now. He had an evil grin on his face.'

'Do you think he could have… ?'

'Sabotaged the order? Yes. My bet is that he is going to do everything to make a fiasco out of this wedding.'

'I'm a bit of a master at improvisational cooking,' I said. 'Let's see what we can do.'

We pushed aside the pastry chef who was about to carry the cake into the hall with great ceremony. It was still unmistakably a Lancaster. Under the bright neon lights, I could even make out little swastikas on the side underneath the cockpit. That was how British pilots notched up the number of German planes they had shot down. No, it really did not seem like a Frau Beckenbender creation at all.

'If we break off the wings like this,' I said, snapping the hardened icing sugar, 'as well as the tail and the fins,' – crack, crack – 'we are left with an interesting new shape.'

'Indisputably,' said Harry. Although he did not sound wholly convinced.

'My God, what are you doing!' shouted the pastry chef as he awoke up out of his horrified trance. 'You're destroying a work of art!'

'Special Branch,' said Harry through gritted teeth. 'Can't you see the swastikas? Use your eyes!'

The cook fell silent. Swastikas are forbidden under German law.

'I was just obeying orders,' he stammered.

'Now,' I said, feeling a rush of a creative energy, 'if we stand it up and wrap it in silver paper — quick get some foil — and put something yellow on top, we can make it look like a torch of freedom.'

'Like the Statue of Liberty,' said Harry.

'That's a disaster!' said the chef. 'It's not how wedding cakes are supposed to look.'

'Well, it's a very special marriage,' I snapped. 'Now find frozen custard, vanilla yellow. Quickly. They're waiting outside.'

We could hear the ascending hum of hungry wedding guests.

The best we could do was peach ice cream straight from the freezer. In truth, it looked a mess. But Frau Beckenbender expected the very worst recipes from me; I would not disappoint her. And the aim was clear. At an Anglo-German wedding – 'Don't mention the war'.

There was some tepid applause as the cake was carried in by two portly apprentices who seemed to have strayed from a Breughel painting.

'What's that supposed to be?' asked von Landauer after I had slipped, panting, into a chair next to him.

'Anything, nothing. You can make what you want out of it. You know how it is with modern art, Ingo.'

'It's a cake.'

'Whatever.'

Frau Beckenbender caught my eye and lifted an empty glass. She mouthed, 'thank-you'. I understood the gesture; a cake as hideously ugly and experimental as this one could only have been devised by me. A back-handed compliment, but better surely than having a marzipan British warplane as the centrepiece of the wedding. I tried to puzzle out how Tom had managed to switch the cake orders. He was even more devious than I thought, and obviously bitterly opposed to this marriage.

'I see Frau Beckenbender likes you,' said von Landauer.

'Yes, we get on. We have a shared interest in potatoes and poverty-cooking.'

'Well, there's nothing very poor about Frau Beckenbender. She's sitting on a fortune.'

Von Landauer noted my astonishment. I was struck dumb. Round us there was the usual clatter of a meal getting underway, and a rubbery chicken was slipped in front of me. Yet I could barely take it in. Frau Beckenbender – rich?

'Yes, there's been a court case pending for years, for as long as she's been my client. Maybe a decade or more. It was a question of whether she or her cousins were the rightful heirs of her uncle's estate. A few weeks ago, the final judgement came through. She is now the owner of six apartment blocks and a couple of flourishing hotels. Not bad, eh?'

'But she has always seemed so poor.'

'That's her charm, isn't it? Your father is a lucky man in so many respects.'

'You know what they say, Ingo. Like father like son.'

'Did I mention that she also now owns some of the best hunting grounds in Germany? Tens of thousands of hectares near the Austrian border. I don't think you're going to have financial problems for much longer.'

My world had turned upside down. Instead of saving my father by constructing a marriage of convenience, my father had saved me by marrying a wealthy woman. It was almost too much to comprehend.

'Did my father know about her money when he started to court her?' I used the old-fashioned word. It seemed appropriate.

'Do you mean did he marry her for her money? I think not. Just look at them.'

And indeed they were gazing at each other like moonstruck adolescents. She picked dust off his lapels and stroked his wrist, hinting at physical intimacy. Between them they had close to 150 years of experience. It did not seem likely that this was a teenage crush, nor that it was a cynical financial deal.

A clinking of fork on glass interrupted my train of thought.

'Sorry to interrupt your eating and drinking, especially your drinking.'

It was Tom. I looked down at my plate. Three courses had come and gone without me noticing. Harry, I realised, was trying to attract my attention with a series of exaggerated winks and subtle waves. He was sitting next to a woman who I vaguely recognised, however his agitation was not stirred by his female companion; but rather by the prospect of Tom hijacking the wedding. I understood Harry's alarm.

'In my role as best man,' said Tom, speaking, of course, in English and gulping after every third word, suggesting he was profoundly drunk. 'In my role (gulp) as best man (gulp), it is my dubious honour (gulp) to wish Bob (gulp) and Whatshername, Mechthild (gulp) – and what kind of name (gulp) is that? – the very best of British luck.'

The gulping was being brought under control, not because Tom was edging towards sobriety but because he was concentrating. Harry was coiled up, ready to spring on top of him like a bodyguard on duty. Everybody else seemed to be bored, rearranging their cutlery or looking at the label of the dessert wine or, in Ingo's case, feeding the dogs with chunks of chicken that had been hidden under a napkin. I realised it was probably my meal since I had not touched it.

'Love is like war,' said Tom, reading uncertainly from notes.

'That is my only consolation. I never thought I would live long enough to preside over an Anglo-German wedding. It is an abomination of nature.'

My father was growing red in the face.

'I used to count Bob as my best friend, but what can I say now? He is collaborating with the enemy.'

Harry and I exchanged glances again. We had only limited options. We could pull the microphone cord out of the plug. We could wrestle Tom to the ground, pretending he was under attack. If we had acted an hour ago, we could perhaps have stolen his false teeth and made the speech incomprehensible.

'Or has my friend – my dear, dear friend (gulp) – become a prisoner of love, which is much much tougher than being a prisoner of war. Believe me, I know.'

Tom patted his artificial leg.

'Bullshit,' I muttered to Ingo who nodded.

'Shall I set the dogs on him?'

'Those softies? They would just end up licking his war wounds.'

'Prisoners of war,' continued Tom, 'are supposed to be treated according to the rules of the Geneva convention. Not that the Germans ever paid much attention to that!'

He glared over at Frau Beckenbender who was sitting up straight, as she had been taught by her nanny so many years ago.

'Prisoners of love are shown no mercy. No food parcels from the Red Cross! No contact with the homeland! They are put into solitary confinement, the key to their cell is thrown away. They cannot tunnel under the perimeter fence to freedom!'

My father was spluttering into his napkin. I hoped he was all right. I wanted to go and pat him on the back but I could see Frau Beckenbender was about to do precisely that.

'Love is full of deceptions, perfidy, subterfuge – it is a coward's game! Real men do not succumb to it. War should be fought in the open, on the field of battle, eye to eye – or, in our case Bob, in the air.'

I could see Dad struggling to his feet. He was, I knew, full of rage. All the signs were there: his eye lids were frantically fluttering, his fists were clenched, his breathing heavy. As a child, I used to be terrified of these outbursts. Tom was barely aware of the brewing storm. He pressed on, taking a full swig of his wine.

'What did we fight the Germans for? Freedom. What is marriage? The opposite of freedom. What is marriage to a German woman? The betrayal of freedom.'

'THAT'S ENOUGH!'

My father grabbed the microphone from Tom and pushed him down onto his seat while simultaneously kicking away his walking stick. Harry nodded approval. It was exactly the technique he would have used.

'Bravo!' shouted Harry, and some of the guests joined in with some hesitant chapping.

'Tom, you were a useless airman, you were a cowardly prisoner and you have built up a false life based on hatred.'

My father was in full throttle.

'I'm ashamed to call you a friend. I was stupid to ask you to be my best man. You wish me and Mechthild nothing but the worst.'

Tom was slumped in his seat. My father put down the microphone but I was close enough to hear him say: 'You make me be ashamed to be English.'

Tom flinched and I started to worry that the public struggle between the two old men would end with a heart attack for one or both of them.

As Dad sat down, Frau Beckenbender touched his wrist. Dad's divorce from Tom was overdue but there was no mistaking the emotional energy that had been pumped into it. For Frau Beckenbender, I knew, it was the ultimate love test; a clear sign that Dad no longer shared Tom's crude, anti-German feelings.

The entire hall, both German and English, clapped and knocked on tables. It was so thunderously loud that the glass rattled and the wires holding the suspended bomber began to swing uncertainly. Harry caught my gaze and shook his head. *No, that would be a disaster.* Tom had sunk into himself like a tortoise withdrawing its head into its shell. I could only imagine his feelings: for sixty years or more Tom had believed that he was speaking for the nation, for the English people. Suddenly, and very publicly, he had been shown that he was hopelessly out of touch. His world would not collapse; he would not change his mind. How could he? He would have to discard the existential myth that he was a British hero, one of an elite, a remarkable person. For a moment, a very brief moment, I felt sorry for him. So, apparently, did my father. Dad got up, took a few paces towards Tom and put an arm round his shoulders. It was a good gesture.

Harry, sensing that the best man was *hors de combat*, pushed his chair back and raised his glass.

'To the bride and groom!'

The call was echoed and a general chaos of scratching furniture, slurred toasts and a half-hearted, drunken attempt to sing the British national anthem ensued. I felt an overwhelming sense of relief.

It took time for everybody to leave. Tradition dictated that the bride and groom should leave early so that the guests could let their hair down. Since most of the guests had no hair to let down, the rules had to be changed. Dad and Mechthild – should I now call her 'Mutti'? – sat near the exit and patiently shook hands as the more elderly guests went home to bed.

Tom was the first to go.

'Bit tired to be honest, Bob.' He patted his artificial leg.

'Great party though,' he added as if nothing had happened.

'Yes,' said Dad with chilly disdain.

'Why don't you take a piece of wedding cake with you,' I chipped in, just to remind him that I was aware of his sabotage attempt.

'No thanks, Sonny Boy,' he said and marched out towards one of the Kurdish drivers.

Slowly, all the guests filtered out.

Ingo had to take the dogs for a late-night walk. ('Believe me,' he whispered, 'your money problems are over.')

Ruediger, smoothing down his kilt, said he had a high-powered dinner to attend with the ambassador to Mozambique. 'We will reschedule its debts, but only if it behaves itself! Money doesn't grow on trees!'

Rose left later on her own and squeezed my hand tightly ('Ring me if you feel homesick').

Tony and Roberta exited in the middle of an argument about who should drive ('Bob,' he said to my father, 'by all means marry a German woman. But not one who thinks she can drive.')

The tipsy, apricot bridesmaids, one of them propped up by a tall, chinless aristocrat, left as a group, declaring their intention to go to a male-stripper club.

The organist left arm-in-arm with a Thai waiter.

Renata had not attended the reception. She had left straight after the wedding saying that Chris had to get ready for a gig with his group, Straight Jacket. I was still quietly satisfied by the understanding we had reached. To have rescued a friendship was a real achievement, for both of us.

As for Harry, he too needed to get out of the wedding party.

'Too much reconciliation,' he said, 'bad for the circulation.'

The real reason though was at his side. I recognised his female companion. It was Gertrud Hanselmeier, the granddaughter of Hitler's last waiter.

'Hello,' I said, 'how's Granddad?'

'Still going strong. Yesterday he was playing battleships in the bath while simultaneously drinking a bottle of rum.'

She smiled, but the smile, and the passion, was reserved for Harry. She was impatient to take him away somewhere.

'Thanks, Harry,' I said, 'you've been a great mate.'

'Forget it,' he said, 'I did my duty for England.'

'Don't be ridiculous.'

'You're right,' he laughed, 'just pulling your leg.' He sidled closer to me. 'Got a story,' he said. 'I'll give you a call later.'

'Harry,' I didn't want to participate in another frantic escapade, 'I don't do Hitler anymore.'

'That's what you think. Wait till you hear what I've got.' Gertrud flexed her impressive muscles and tugged him away.

'Come on,' she cooed, 'we have some serious business to discuss.'

Harry raised his eyebrows at me and let himself be led off.

Frau Beckenbender supervised the caterers as they stashed away the dirty glasses and covertly sipped from half-empty bottles.

Dad and I went outside to gulp some fresh air but it was too cold to linger. We found a bench inside near an exhibit of the Berlin Wall. Dad looked exhausted.

'Where are you going on your honeymoon?' I asked. 'Not taking the Tuareg caravan, I hope.'

I could not imagine Frau Beckenbender adapting to the cramped, smelly space. In fact, I could not picture the caravan ever leaving Dad's garden. It was the kind of vehicle you see dumped in corners of grubby farmyards, used as a chicken coop.

'No, the caravanning days are over, Son.'

'Anyway, you're rich now. You could go to Capri.'

'Stop talking about money, Son, you behave as if it's the only thing in the world.'

'Well, that's how you were talking a few months ago when you couldn't pay your cleaning lady.' I remembered the helter-skelter of events since Dad had first pushed the panic button. It had not been easy for either of us. And yet here we were chatting as father and son should.

'Aye, money is the biggest thing in the world when you don't have it.' He shook his head slowly as if he were an Oriental sage.

'Where are you going to live, Dad? England or Germany?'

'Don't right know. We could try a bit of both.'

'Meaning?'

'Majorca.' The island was, of course, firmly split between the British and the Germans. I quite liked the idea of that. They could eat fish and chips on one day of the week, pork knuckle on the next. Or, if they borrowed a few of my recipes, mix up the two national cuisines in some unholy mess. And I could visit them. It had been a long time since I had a holiday.

'You'd be welcome, of course,' said Dad, seeming to read my thoughts. 'For a short while.'

We sat in silence. I wanted a cigarette but did not light up. My father, I could see, wanted a whiskey but did not attempt to find one. We were locked in mutual self-denial, like Trappist monks.

'What I meant to tell you, Dad…' I began. I saw his eyes coasting over the tables in search of a bottle of scotch; his resolve was wavering. Then his gaze locked with that of Frau Beckenbender. A secret telepathic message seemed to pass between them and Dad concentrated again on our conversation, the scotch apparently forgotten. Dad's new wife, I could see, would keep him quietly under control. And a good thing too.

'I wanted to tell you,' I said, picking up my train of thought, 'that I'm very proud of you. What you did today. I mean everything: allowing yourself to fall in love, get married, question yourself, slap down Tom. Especially slapping down Tom.'

'Aye,' said Dad, after what seemed to be a pause of several decades. 'Well, I'm proud of you too. But I don't want anymore of this sentimental balderdash. People will think you've gone soft in the head.'

And that's just about as good as it gets.

MORE KETCHUP
THAN SALSA
CONFESSIONS OF A TENERIFE BARMAN

JOE CAWLEY

More Ketchup Than Salsa

Confessions of a Tenerife Barman

Joe Cawley

£8.99

978-1-84024-501-1

Winner of the British Guild of Travel Writers Award for Best Narrative Book 2007

When Joe and his girlfriend Joy decide to trade in their life on a cold Lancashire fish market to run a bar in the Tenerife sunshine, they anticipate a paradise of sea, sand and siestas. Little do they expect their foreign fantasy to turn out to be about as exotic as Grimsby on a wet Monday morning.

Amidst a host of eccentric locals, homesickness and the occasional cockroach infestation, pint-pulling novices Joe and Joy struggle with 'Brits abroad' culture and learn that, although the skies might be bluer, the grass is definitely not always greener.

More Ketchup than Salsa lifts the lid on the morning-afters as well as the night-befores of life in a busy holiday resort. A must-read for anybody who has ever dreamed about jetting off to sunnier climes.

Joe Cawley has written for *The Sunday Times*, *The Guardian*, *The Independent*, *The Observer*, *The New York Post* and *Condé Nast Traveler*. He lives in Tenerife.

'you'll find plenty here to make you either squirm or laugh heartily out loud'
LIVING SPAIN magazine

'Spiked with humour and sharp observation, this is a reality check for those who dream of running an expats' pub in Spain. It's a wry reminder that the grass isn't always greener on the sunny side of the street – or, indeed, on the other side of the bar'
Peter Kerr

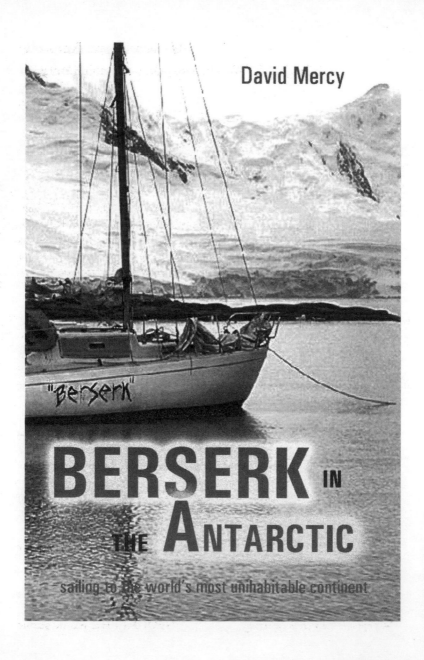

David Mercy

"Berserk"

BERSERK IN THE ANTARCTIC

sailing to the world's most unihabitable continent

Berserk in the Antarctic
Sailing to the World's Most Uninhabitable Continent
David Mercy
£7.99

978-1-84024-479-3

'This is suicide!' Manuel screamed frantically.

So begins an amazing true story of a journey to Antarctica in a 27-foot sailing boat. After travelling through South America to Tierra del Fuego, the only continent David had never visited beckoned to him across treacherous waters. Ships booked for scientific expeditions wouldn't take him, and tourist cruises didn't appeal. Then he saw a little boat in the harbour, its name hand-painted in red on the hull: *Berserk*.

Together with a 'crazy Viking' and a down-on-his-luck Argentinian, the author set sail to follow Shackleton's voyage with little idea of the tumultuous storms, mishaps and emergencies that loomed on the journey to the world's coldest and most inaccessible continent. He brilliantly recounts their experience of the huge waves, the bleak darkness and the delicate balance of personalities where a mutiny was always in the air.

David Mercy is a director and producer of independent films. He has travelled on every continent and lives in Los Angeles, California.

'Some extreme adventure books strike you as so off-the-wall outrageous that you can't believe anybody would take that kind of risk, and you just can't stop turning the pages. David Mercy's Berserk *falls into this category with a vengeance... it should probably come with a consumer warning: Don't try this at home'*
OFFSHORE magazine

'If ever a travel book should come with a "don't try this at home" warning, this is it'
ADVENTURE TRAVEL magazine

'always one wave from capsizing'   GEOGRAPHICAL magazine

A Chateau Of One's Own

Restoration Misadventures in France

SAM JUNEAU

A Chateau of One's Own

Restoration Misadventures in France

Sam Juneau

£7.99

978-1-84024-553-0

Sam and Bud were ordinary first-time homebuyers in their early thirties. Their intention in moving to France was to create a simple life and spend more time with their children. The home they actually bought was an impressive seventeenth-century chateau in the Loire valley with over thirty rooms, 156 windows and 40 acres of land.

With only modest savings, the couple launched the challenging project of restoring this crumbling monster of a building to its former glory and opening a bed and breakfast in the process. This is the hilarious story of behind the scenes at a B&B that required constant disaster relief: think *Fawlty Towers* in an extraordinary setting.

A Chateau of One's Own will appeal to those like Sam and Bud who want to escape from the rat race, who work hard and have hardly enough time to play. It's the perfect read for anyone considering a grandiose home makeover project and for all of us who dream of a life in France.

Sam Juneau was born in New Orleans and is a television producer and writer in the UK and the US. He and his wife live in France with their children and 22 cats.

'a refreshing warts-and-all account of what follows from that impulse buy: from hilarious encounters with French doctors... to nightmare bed-and-breakfast guests'
SUNDAY EXPRESS

'the perfect read for anyone considering a grandiose home makeover project and for all of us who dream of a life in France'
LIVING FRANCE

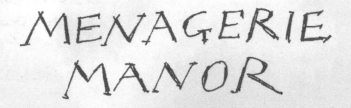

MENAGERIE MANOR

Gerald Durrell

Menagerie Manor
Gerald Durrell
£7.99

978-1-84024-553-0

'Most children at the tender age of six or so are generally full of the most impractical schemes for becoming policemen, firemen or engine drivers when they grow up... I knew exactly what I was going to do: I was going to have my own zoo.'

This is the hugely entertaining account of how the much-loved conservationist and author, Gerald Durrell, fulfilled his lifelong ambition by founding his own private sanctuary for endangered species in Jersey with the help of an enduring wife, a selfless staff and a reluctant bank manager.

With a foreword by Lee Durrell, Honorary Director of the Durrell Wildlife Conservation Trust, this book about the trials and wonders of living in the middle of a zoo is a classic that will continue to bring pleasure to those who grew up reading Durrell, and deserves a whole new readership.

Gerald Durrell lived in Corfu with his family as a boy and immediately became fascinated by the island's natural history; these years are famously documented in *My Family and Other Animals*. His lifetime's work began with expeditions to collect endangered animals from all over the world and bring them to his breeding sanctuary. This evolved into the Durrell Wildlife Conservation Trust, which operates conservation programmes worldwide, carrying on Gerald Durrell's mission to save species from extinction.

'You can't deny that there are some species that now exist because of him'
Craig Bennett, FRIENDS OF THE EARTH

'It is largely thanks to Gerald Durrell's eccentric vision that zoos... now play an important role in conservation' THE TIMES

'Highly entertaining' SUNDAY TELEGRAPH

'A renegade who was right... He was truly a man before his time'
Sir David Attenborough

www.summersdale.com